THE FATHERS
OF THE CHURCH

A NEW TRANSLATION

VOLUME 149

THE FATHERS OF THE CHURCH

A NEW TRANSLATION

EDITORIAL BOARD

David G. Hunter
Boston College
Editorial Director

Paul M. Blowers
Emmanuel Christian Seminary

William E. Klingshirn
The Catholic University of America

Aaron Butts
The Catholic University of America

Joseph T. Lienhard, S.J.
Fordham University

Andrew Cain
University of Colorado

Michael W. Heintz
University of Notre Dame

Mark DelCogliano
University of St. Thomas

Wendy Mayer
University of Divinity (Australia)

Robert A. Kitchen
Regina, Saskatchewan

Trevor Lipscombe
Director, The Catholic University of America Press

FORMER EDITORIAL DIRECTORS
Ludwig Schopp, Roy J. Deferrari, Bernard M. Peebles,
Hermigild Dressler, O.F.M., Thomas P. Halton

Carole Monica C. Burnett, *Staff Editor*

ST. JOHN CHRYSOSTOM

CONSOLATION TO STAGIRIUS

Translated by

ROBERT G. T. EDWARDS

THE CATHOLIC UNIVERSITY OF AMERICA PRESS
Washington, D.C.

Copyright @ 2024
THE CATHOLIC UNIVERSITY OF AMERICA PRESS
All rights reserved
Printed in Canada

The paper used in this publication meets the minimum
requirements of the American National Standards for
Information Science—Permanence of Paper for Printed
Library Materials, ANSI z39.48 - 1984.
∞

ISBN 978-0-8132-3922-4

CIP data is available from the
Library of Congress.

CONTENTS

Dedication	vi
Acknowledgments	vii
Abbreviations	xi
Select Bibliography	xiii

Introduction	3
The Occasion of the *Consolation to Stagirius*	3
Syrian Asceticism	6
Despondency, Consolation, and Ancient Medicine	10
Divine Providence, Philanthropy, and Human Suffering	15
Biblical Interpretation	19
Notes on the Translation and Text	24

CONSOLATION TO STAGIRIUS

Book I	29
Book II	69
Book III	109

INDICES

General Index	151
Index of Holy Scripture	154

To all those who through the years have
offered me consolation

ACKNOWLEDGMENTS

As this project of translating John Chrysostom's *Consolation to Stagirius* comes to a close, the overwhelming feeling is that of gratitude. While many were of immediate assistance, there were many more than these who came before and who have allowed, in the first place, for the work to be translated. Of course, that priest of Syrian Antioch who became the short-lived archbishop of Constantinople (later to be exiled in Armenia, where he breathed his last) is owed the greatest debt. And yet it is not really his work that I am translating—at least not something written by his own hand. The text was most likely taken down by a stenographer or scribe; copied time and time again throughout the centuries; translated into various languages; edited "scientifically" in the seventeenth through the nineteenth centuries; commented on by scholars of the twentieth and twenty-first centuries—it is to all these who put in so many hours (many more than myself) to whom gratitude is owed. Without these individuals, most of whom are unknown to us, there would be nothing to translate, and no earlier work on which I could rely. That I could play a small part in the transmission of this text is, for me, reason for thanksgiving.

Of course, there is also a sense of trepidation. Those who came before were often consummate experts. For example, in the Anglophone world, Sir Henry Savile, who was responsible for the first modern printed edition of *Chrysostomi Opera Omnia*, was also the tutor of a young Queen Elizabeth I, Warden of Merton College, Oxford, provost of Eton College, translator of Tacitus, and one of the team of translators of King James' Authorized Version of the Bible. What arrogance—what folly!—to attempt to follow up his work, even in this humble way.

This is not to mention the many others, in English and other modern languages, who have contributed to our knowledge about this early work of John Chrysostom. Despite this trepidation (and the knowledge that the first to translate a work into any given language paints a target on his or her back), the overwhelming feeling at having completed this translation is one of gratitude to those who have done the much harder preceding work. What is offered in this volume, then, is given in the spirit of contributing humbly to a tradition of the reception of John Chrysostom's work—one which has endured for more than a century and a half. May this tradition endure.

On a personal note, I have chosen to dedicate this translation to those who have over the years offered me some form of consolation. It is not that I, more than others, am in special need of consolation. We all require comfort at various points in our lives, and more often than we would hope. As I understand it, consolation means to "speak the truth in love" (Eph 4.15) in contexts of grief, loss, or sadness. To speak the truth in love is no simple task, as neither truth nor love are easily acquired—and rarely do they coincide. Consolation does not, however, require *profound* truths (such as are offered by John Chrysostom and other early Christian consolers). Often simple ones are the best. At the same time, consolatory truths require true love: an unrelenting desire for the good of the other.

I have been gifted with many able consolers in my life, some of whom I mention here (forgive me if I have left you off the list). Within my family, these include my parents, grandparents, brothers, nieces and nephews, in-laws, my wife Kerensa, and our daughters. Among my friends and companions on the journey are (in no particular order) Ken Moser, Sean Love, Jeff Hayashi, Eric Thurston, Chris Ley, Jamie Turner, Jennie and Luke Potter, Kacie and Patrick Klamm, Paul Wheatley, Jeremiah Coogan, and many, many others. May the Lord bless you and keep you.

The translation itself took shape over a number of years. It began as a working draft during my doctoral research, as I wrote on John Chrysostom's teaching on providence and its dependence on the exegesis of biblical narratives. This research was eventually published as *Providence and Narrative in the Theology of John Chrysostom* (Cambridge University Press, 2022). The translation mostly lay dormant during my time as a researcher at the University of Göttingen, though I did work on it during that time in fits and spurts. Finally, it has reached completion at the Brisbane School of Theology, one of the constituent colleges of the Australian College of Theology. I have therefore accrued many academic debts. The first of these is to Blake Leyerle, that consummate mentor and encourager, who supervised my thesis. At one time she had plans to translate the *Consolation to Stagirius* herself, but generously ceded that task to me. Thanks also go to faculty and my doctoral colleagues at the University of Notre Dame and then at the University of Göttingen. I am grateful too for the support of my new colleagues at the Brisbane School of Theology, especially Andrew Prince, who read the bulk of the manuscript before it went to press. Finally, many thanks are due to Carole Monica Burnett, the editor of the Fathers of the Church series, for her plenteous advice, encouragement, and endurance (read: patience).

Thanks are also due to institutions for the opportunity they afforded by way of funding and other institutional support: namely, the University of Notre Dame, the Social Sciences and Humanities Research Council of Canada, the University of Göttingen, the Humboldt Foundation, and the Brisbane School of Theology.

ABBREVIATIONS

Anom. [*De incomp.*]	John Chrysostom, *Contra anomoeos de incomprehensibili Dei natura*
ANRW	*Aufstieg und Niedergang der römischen Welt*
CH	*Church History*
CP	*Classical Philology*
Demetr.	John Chrysostom, *Ad Demetrium de compunctione*
Diab.	John Chrysostom, *De diabolo tentatore*
Dial.	Palladius of Hierapolis, *Dialogus de vita Johannis Chrysostomi*
GOTR	*Greek Orthodox Theological Review*
Hist. eccl.	*Historia ecclesiastica*
Hist. rel.	Theodoret of Cyrrhus, *Historia religiosa*
Hom. 1 Tim.	John Chrysostom, *In epistulam i ad Timotheum homiliae*
Hom. Gen.	John Chrysostom, *Homiliae in Genesim*
Hom. Matt.	John Chrysostom, *Homiliae in Matthaeum*
Hom. Nat.	Nemesius of Emesa, *De hominum natura*
JLA	*Journal of Late Antiquity*
LXX	Septuagint
MT	Masoretic Text
OCP	*Orientalia Christiana Periodica*
OG	Old Greek
Paralyt.	John Chrysostom, *In paralyticum demissum per tectum*
PG	Patrologia Graeca
Sacer.	John Chrysostom, *De sacerdotio*

ABBREVIATIONS

SC	Sources Chrétiennes. Paris: Cerf.
Scand.	John Chrysostom, *Ad eos qui scandalizati sunt* (*de providentia Dei*)
SJT	*Scottish Journal of Theology*
Stag.	John Chrysostom, *Ad Stagirium a daemone vexatum*
Stat.	John Chrysostom, *De statuis ad populum Antiochenum*
StPatr	*Studia Patristica*
VC	*Vigiliae Christianae*

SELECT BIBLIOGRAPHY

Algra, Keimpe. "Stoic Theology." In *The Cambridge Companion to the Stoics,* edited by Brad Inwood, 153–78. Cambridge: Cambridge University Press, 2006.
Amand de Mendieta, Emmanuel. "L'amplification d'un thème socratique et stoïcien dans l'avant dernier traité de Jean Chrysostome." *Byzantion* 36 (1966): 353–81.
Amirav, Hagit. *Rhetoric and Tradition: John Chrysostom on Noah and the Flood.* Leuven: Peeters, 2003.
Baltussen, Han. "Introduction." In *Greek and Roman Consolations: Eight Studies of a Tradition and its Afterlife,* edited by Han Baltussen, xiii–xx. Swansea: Classical Press of Wales, 2013.
Bardolle, M.-A. "Tristesse (*athumia*) et thérapeutique spirituelle dans l'*Exhortation à Stagire* de Chrysostome." *Lettre de Ligugé* 241, no. 3 (1987): 6–19.
Baur, Chrysostomus. *Heilige Johannes Chrysostomus und seine Zeit.* 2 volumes. Munich: Hueber, 1929–1930. [English translation: *John Chrysostom and His Time.* 2 volumes. Translated by M. Gonzaga. Westminster, MD: Newman, 1959–1960.]
Bénatouïl, Thomas. "How Industrious can Zeus be?" In *God and Cosmos in Stoicism,* edited by Ricardo Salles, 23–45. Oxford: Oxford University Press, 2009.
Bergjan, Silke-Petra. *Der fürsorgende Gott: Der Begriff der ΠΡΟΝΟΙΑ Gottes in der apologetischen Literatur der Alten Kirche.* Berlin: De Gruyter, 2002.
Brändle, Rudolf. *Johannes Chrysostomus: Bischof, Reformer, Märtyrer.* Stuttgart: Kohlhammer, 1999.
Broc-Schmezer, Catherine. "Lectures et récritures chrysostomiennes des premiers chapitres de la Genèse." *Graphè* 17 (2008): 95–125.
Brottier, Laurence. "Un jeu de mots intraduisible: Le combat entre *thumos* et *athumia* dans des homélies de Jean Chrysostome." *Revue de Philologie, de Littérature et d'Histoire Anciennes* 72, no. 2 (1998): 189–204.
Carter, Robert E. "The Image of God in Man and Woman according to Severian of Gabala and the Antiochene Tradition." *OCP* 69, no. 1 (2003): 163–78.
Clark, Elizabeth A. "John Chrysostom and the 'Subintroductae.'" *CH* 46, no. 2 (1977): 171–85.
Crépey, Cyrille. "Le vrai sens de la littéralité de l'exégèse dans les Homélies

sur la Genèse de Jean Chrysostome: illustration à partir de l'exégèse de Gn 1:1." *StPatr* 47 (2010): 249–54.

Dihle, Albrecht. "Liberté et destin dans l'antiquité tardive." *Revue de Théologie et de Philosophie* 121 (1989): 129–47.

Dragas, George D. "St. John Chrysostom's Doctrine of God's Providence." *Ekklesiastikos Pharos* 57 (1957): 375–406.

Dragona-Monachou, Myrto. "Divine Providence in the Philosophy of Empire." *ANRW* II 36, no. 7 (1994): 4417–90.

Edwards, Robert G. T. "Divine Incomprehensibility and Human Faith in John Chrysostom." *VC* 76, no. 4 (2022): 434–62.

———. "The Gospel of John and Antiochene Christology: The Diverging Cases of Theodore of Mopsuestia and John Chrysostom." *SJT* 74, no. 4 (2021): 333–45.

———. "Grammar in the School of Diodore of Tarsus: An Institutional Context for the Transfer of Exegetical Knowledge." In *Knowledge Construction in Late Antiquity*, edited by Monika Amsler, 257–81. Berlin: De Gruyter, 2023.

———. *Providence and Narrative in the Theology of John Chrysostom*. Cambridge: Cambridge University Press, 2022.

———. "Providence, Ethics, and Exempla: Reassessing the Stoicism of John Chrysostom's *Quod nemo laeditur nisi a se ipso*." In *Greek and Byzantine Philosophical Exegesis*, edited by J. B. Wallace and A. Despotis, 217–43. Paderborn: Schöningh, 2022.

Finn, Douglas. "Sympathetic Philosophy: The Christian Response to Suffering according to John Chrysostom's Commentary on Job." In *Suffering and Evil in Early Christian Thought*, edited by Nonna Verna Harrison and David G. Hunter, 97–119. Grand Rapids, MI: Baker Academic, 2016.

Gill, Christopher. "Ancient Psychotherapy." *Journal of the History of Ideas* 46, no. 3 (1985): 307–25.

———. "Philosophical Therapy as Preventative Psychological Medicine." In *Mental Disorders in the Classical World*, edited by William V. Harris, 339–60. Leiden: Brill, 2013.

Gregg, Robert C. *Consolation Philosophy: Greek and Christian Paideia in Basil and the Two Gregories*. Cambridge, MA: Philadelphia Patristic Foundation, 1975.

Guinot, Jean-Noël. "Les exempla bibliques dans l'Ad Stagirium de Jean Chrysostome: proposition d'une clef de lecture." In *Giovanni Crisostomo: Oriente e occidente tra IV e V secolo, XXXIII Incontro di Studiosi dell'Antichità Cristiana, Roma, 6–8 Maggio 2004*, 163–83. Rome: Institutum patristicum Augustinianum, 2005.

Hainthaler, Theresia. "Pronoia bei Johannes Chrysostomus in *De providentia* und seinen Briefen an Olympias." In *Pronoia. The Providence of God. Die Vorsehung Gottes. Forscher aus dem Osten und Westen Europas an den Quellen des gemeinsamen Glaubens: Studientagung Warschau, 30. August–4. September*

2017, edited by T. Hainthaler, F. Mali, and M. Lenkaityte Ostermann, 145–61. Innsbruck: Tyrolia, 2019.

Hall, Christopher A. "Nature Wild and Tame in St. John Chrysostom's *On the Providence of God.*" In *Ancient and Postmodern Christianity: Paleo-Orthodoxy in the 21st Century: Essays in Honor of Thomas C. Oden,* edited by Kenneth Tanner and Christopher A. Hall, 23–37. Downers Grove, IL: InterVarsity, 2002.

Hill, Robert C. "Akribeia: A Principle of Chrysostom's Exegesis." *Colloquium* 14, no. 1 (1981): 32–36.

———. "On Looking Again at Sunkatabasis." *Prudentia* 13 (1981): 3–11.

———. *Reading the Old Testament in Antioch.* Leiden: Brill, 2005.

Hubbell, Harry M. "Chrysostom and Rhetoric." *CP* 19, no. 3 (1924): 261–76.

Illert, Martin. *Johannes Chrysostomus und das antiochenische-syrische Mönchtum. Studien zu Theologie, Rhetorik und Kirchenpolitik im antiochenischen Schrifttum des Johannes Chrysostomus.* Zürich: Pano, 2000.

Katos, Demetrios S. *Palladius of Helenopolis: The Origenist Advocate.* Oxford: Oxford University Press, 2011.

Kecskeméti, Judit. "Exégèse Chrysostomienne et exégèse engagée." *StPatr* 22 (1989): 136–47.

Kelly, J. N. D. *Golden Mouth: The Story of John Chrysostom—Ascetic, Preacher, Bishop.* Ithaca, NY: Cornell University Press, 1995.

Lai, Pak-Wah. "The *Imago Dei* and Salvation among the Antiochenes: A Comparison of John Chrysostom with Theodore of Mopsuestia." *StPatr* 67 (2013): 393–402.

Laird, Raymond. *Mindset, Moral Choice and Sin in the Anthropology of John Chrysostom.* Strathfield, NSW, Australia: St Pauls, 2012.

Leyerle, Blake. "The Etiology of Sorrow and its Therapeutic Benefits in the Preaching of John Chrysostom." *JLA* 8, no. 2 (2015): 368–85.

———. *The Narrative Shape of Emotion in the Preaching of John Chrysostom.* Berkeley: University of California Press, 2020.

———. "The Strategic Use of Fear in the Preaching of John Chrysostom." In *Social Control in Late Antiquity: The Violence of Small Worlds,* edited by Kate Cooper and Jamie Wood, 173–87. Cambridge: Cambridge University Press, 2020.

———. *Theatrical Shows and Ascetic Lives: John Chrysostom's Attack on Spiritual Marriage.* Berkeley: University of California Press, 2001.

Louth, Andrew. "Pagans and Christians on Providence." In *Text and Culture in Late Antiquity: Inheritance, Authority and Change,* edited by J. H. D. Scourfield and Anna Chahoud, 279–97. Swansea: Classical Press of Wales, 2007.

Malingrey, Anne-Marie, ed. *Jean Chrysostome: Sur la providence de Dieu.* SC 79. Paris: Cerf, 2000.

———, ed. *Jean Chrysostome: Sur le sacerdoce (Dialogue et Homélie).* SC 272. Paris: Cerf, 1980.

Mayer, Wendy, ed. *The Cult of the Saints.* Popular Patristics Series. Volume 31. Crestwood, NY: St Vladimir's Seminary Press, 2006.

———. *The Homilies of St John Chrysostom: Provenance, Reshaping the Foundations.* Rome: Orientalium, 2005.

———. "The Making of a Saint: John Chrysostom in Early Historiography." In *Chrysostomosbilder in 1600 Jahren: Facetten der Wirkungsgeschichte eines Kirchenvaters,* edited by Martin Wallraff and Rudolf Brändle, 39–59. Berlin: De Gruyter, 2008.

———. "Monasticism at Antioch and Constantinople in the Late Fourth Century: A Case of Exclusivity or Diversity?" In *Prayer and Spirituality in the Early Church,* volume 1, edited by Pauline Allen, Raymond Canning, Lawrence Cross, and Janelle B. Caiger, 275–88. Everton Park, Qld., Australia: Centre for Early Christian Studies, Australian Catholic University, 1998.

———. "Patronage, Pastoral Care and the Role of the Bishop at Antioch." *VC* 55, no. 1 (2001): 58–70.

———. "The Persistence in Late Antiquity of Medico-Philosophical Psychic Therapy." *JLA* 8, no. 2 (2015): 337–51.

———. "Shaping the Sick Soul: Reshaping the Identity of John Chrysostom." In *Christians Shaping Identity from the Roman Empire to Byzantium: Studies Inspired by Pauline Allen,* edited by Geoffrey Dunn and Wendy Mayer, 140–64. Leiden: Brill, 2015.

———. "What does it mean to say that John Chrysostom was a monk?" *StPatr* 41 (2006): 451–55.

Miller, Samantha L. *Chrysostom's Devil: Demons, the Will, and Virtue in Patristic Soteriology.* Downers Grove, IL: InterVarsity, 2020.

———. "Chrysostom's Monks as Living Exhortations to Poverty and the Rich Life." *GOTR* 58 (2013): 79–98.

Mitchell, Margaret M. *The Heavenly Trumpet: John Chrysostom and the Art of Pauline Interpretation.* Tübingen: Mohr Siebeck, 2000.

Neil, Bronwen. "Divine Providence and Free Will in Gregory of Nyssa and His Theological Milieu." *Phronema* 27, no. 2 (2012): 35–51.

Nowak, Edward. *Le chrétien devant la souffrance. Étude sur la pensée de Jean Chrysostome.* Paris: Beauchesne, 1972.

Parry, Ken. "Fate, Free Choice, and Divine Providence from the Neoplatonists to John of Damascus." In *The Cambridge Intellectual History of Byzantium,* edited by Anthony Kaldellis and Niketas Siniossoglou, 341–60. Cambridge: Cambridge University Press, 2017.

Patrich, Joseph. *Sabas, Leader of Palestinian Monasticism: A Comparative Study in Eastern Monasticism, Fourth to Seventh Centuries.* Washington, DC: Dumbarton Oaks, 1995.

Pigott, Justin M. "Capital Crimes: Deconstructing John's 'Unnecessary Severity' in Managing the Clergy at Constantinople." In *Revisioning John Chrysostom: New Approaches, New Perspectives,* edited by Chris de Wet and Wendy Mayer, 733–78. Leiden: Brill, 2019.

———. *New Rome Wasn't Built in a Day: Rethinking Councils and Controversy at Early Constantinople 381–451.* Turnhout: Brepols, 2019.

Rylaarsdam, David. *John Chrysostom on Divine Pedagogy: The Coherence of his Theology and Preaching.* Oxford: Oxford University Press, 2014.
Schatkin, Margaret A. *John Chrysostom as Apologist: With Special Reference to De incomprehensibili, Quod nemo laeditur, Ad eos qui scandalizati sunt, and Adversus oppugnatores vitae monasticae.* Thessaloniki: Patriarchikon Hidryma Paterikōn Meletōn, 1987.
Schäublin, Christoph. *Untersuchungen zu Methode und Herkunft der antiochenischen Exegese.* Cologne: Hanstein, 1974.
Scourfield, J. H. D. "Towards a Genre of Consolation." In *Greek and Roman Consolations: Eight Studies of a Tradition and its Afterlife,* edited by Han Baltussen, 1–36. Swansea: Classical Press of Wales, 2013.
Sharples, R. W. "Nemesius of Emesa and Some Theories of Divine Providence." *VC* 37, no. 2 (1983): 141–56.
———. "Threefold Providence: The History and Background of a Doctrine." *Bulletin of the Institute of Classical Studies. Supplement, 78: Ancient Approaches to Plato's Timaeus* (2003): 107–27.
Sharples, R. W., and Philip Van der Eijk, trans. *Nemesius: On the Nature of Man.* Liverpool: Liverpool University Press, 2008.
Stewart, Columba. "The Ascetic Taxonomy of Antioch and Edessa at the Emergence of Monasticism." *Adamantius* 19 (2013): 207–21.
Tiersch, Claudia. *Johannes Chrysostomus in Konstantinopel (398–404). Weltsicht und Wirken eines Bischofs in der Hauptstadt des Oströmischen Reiches.* Tübingen: Mohr Siebeck, 2002.
Tonias, Demetrios E. *Abraham in the Works of John Chrysostom.* Minneapolis: Fortress, 2014.
Uleyn, Arnold. "La doctrine morale de saint Jean Chrysostome dans le Commentaire sur saint Matthieu et ses affinités avec la diatribe." *Revue de l'Université d'Ottawa* 27, no. 1–2 (1957): 6–25, 99–140.
van de Paverd, Frans. *St. John Chrysostom, The Homilies on the Statues: An Introduction.* Rome: Orientalium, 1991.
Volp, Ulrich. "'That Unclean Spirit Has Assaulted You from the Very Beginning': John Chrysostom and Suicide." *StPatr* 47 (2010): 273–86.
Wright, Jessica. "Between Despondency and the Demon: Diagnosing and Treating Spiritual Disorders in John Chrysostom's *Letter to Stageirios.*" *JLA* 8, no. 2 (2015): 352–67.

INTRODUCTION

INTRODUCTION

The Occasion of the Consolation to Stagirius

Almost everything that we know about John Chrysostom's life comes from the time he spent in Constantinople as archbishop and his subsequent exile. Consecrated as bishop of that city in 397, he was judged by Theophilus, bishop of Alexandria, to be complicit in the ill-defined "Origenist" heresy, ended up on the bad side of the empress Eudoxia, and was subsequently sent into exile (in 403), where he died four years later.[1] In addition to the accounts of the church historians Socrates and Sozomen, two of John's supporters—Palladius of Hierapolis and an anonymous writer ("Pseudo-Martyrius")— penned works in defense of him within just a few years of his deposition and the subsequent dispersal of his followers.[2]

---

1. For modern biographical accounts, see J. N. D. Kelly, *Golden Mouth: The Story of John Chrysostom—Ascetic, Preacher, Bishop* (Ithaca, NY: Cornell University Press, 1995); Rudolf Brändle, *Johannes Chrysostomus: Bischof, Reformer, Märtyrer* (Stuttgart: Kohlhammer, 1999). The classic, now outdated account is Chrysostomus Baur, *Heilige Johannes Chrysostomus und seine Zeit*, 2 vols. (Munich: Hueber, 1929–1930) [English translation: *John Chrysostom and His Time*, 2 vols., trans. M. Gonzaga (Westminster, MD: Newman, 1959–1960)]. For two competing scholarly accounts of these tumultuous later years, see Claudia Tiersch, *Johannes Chrysostomus in Konstantinopel (398–404). Weltsicht und Wirken eines Bischofs in der Hauptstadt des Oströmischen Reiches* (Tübingen: Mohr Siebeck, 2002); and Justin M. Pigott, "Capital Crimes: Deconstructing John's 'Unnecessary Severity' in Managing the Clergy at Constantinople," in *Revisioning John Chrysostom: New Approaches, New Perspectives*, ed. Chris de Wet and Wendy Mayer (Leiden: Brill, 2019), 733–78, and his fuller treatment in *New Rome Wasn't Built in a Day: Rethinking Councils and Controversy at Early Constantinople 381–451* (Turnhout: Brepols, 2019).

2. On Palladius's own bent, see Demetrios S. Katos, *Palladius of Helenopolis: The Origenist Advocate* (Oxford: Oxford University Press, 2011).

INTRODUCTION

John himself also wrote a series of letters from his exile that help historians to fill out this picture. We therefore have quite a full picture of Chrysostom's episcopal ministry in Constantinople and his ever-deeper exile into Pontus and then Armenia.[3]

This later period of John's life, however, is less relevant to the work translated in this volume because he most likely wrote to the monk Stagirius during the earlier part of his ministry, when he was a deacon or a priest. The best information about this stage of his life, including the composition of the *Consolation to Stagirius*, comes from the *Ecclesiastical History* of Socrates of Constantinople, who wrote in the middle of the fifth century. With respect to the *Consolation to Stagirius*, he writes, "Not long after John obtained from Meletius the dignity of the diaconate, he composed discourses *On the Priesthood* and *To Stagirius*, as well as *On Incomprehensibility*, and *On Those who Cohabit*."[4] Although Socrates makes enough mistakes in John's biography before his time in Constantinople that his claims must be taken with a grain of salt,[5] there are other reasons for thinking that the *Consolation to Stagirius* was indeed written during John's diaconate. First, beginning in early modernity, scholars have usually assumed that Chrysostom's "ascetic" works were written at the beginning of his ecclesiastical career, soon after he had given up a monastic life. While this can hardly be taken as a rule,[6] it is not unlikely that Chrysostom would have had more time for writing during his diaconal ministry than after his ordination as a priest, when he began

---

3. On the reliability of these various accounts, see Wendy Mayer, "The Making of a Saint: John Chrysostom in Early Historiography," in *Chrysostomosbilder in 1600 Jahren: Facetten der Wirkungsgeschichte eines Kirchenvaters*, ed. Martin Wallraff and Rudolf Brändle (Berlin: De Gruyter, 2008), 39–59.

4. Socrates, *Hist. eccl.* 6.3.

5. For example, that he was ordained by the rival Nicene bishop of Antioch, Evagrius, when it is well known from Chrysostom's own sermons that he served under Meletius's successor, Flavian.

6. Wendy Mayer is rightly skeptical of many of the criteria whereby early modern scholars judged the settings of John's writings, especially his sermons: *The Homilies of St John Chrysostom: Provenance, Reshaping the Foundations* (Rome: Orientalium, 2005).

to preach more frequently. Preparing and preaching sermons would have consumed much of his time as a priest in Antioch, and then later as Bishop of Constantinople, when his time was also increasingly consumed with administrative and political responsibilities.[7]

Even if the *Consolation to Stagirius* was not written during his diaconate, it almost certainly was written when he lived in Antioch—and thus during either his diaconal or his sacerdotal ministry. Whereas asceticism was not well established in Constantinople and its environs around 400, it was already prevalent throughout Syria. In fact, the ascetic practice that Chrysostom alludes to in some of his works resembles closely what we know of Syrian monasticism from other sources (on which, see below). Another hint as to the treatise's Antiochene provenance comes from its close textual relationship—that is, a near-verbatim copy of several sentences—with one of the *Homilies on the Statues*. And this latter series of sermons can be firmly dated to Lent 387 in Antioch.[8] Although it is possible that Chrysostom brought manuscripts of his *Homilies on the Statues* with him to Constantinople and then copied from them in his *Consolation to Stagirius*, the close textual relationship between the two—whatever the direction of dependence might be—indicates that they were probably composed around the same time. Therefore, although there is no way of pinpointing precisely the date of his writing of the *Consolation to Stagirius*, it was most likely written either during his diaconal ministry or early in his presbyterate in Antioch, and thus sometime in the first three quarters of the 380s.

To whom is this treatise addressed? Unfortunately, no other information about this particular Stagirius survives. We do, however, learn something about him in the treatise itself, even apart from his ailments. Stagirius appears to come from a well-off family, perhaps in Antioch: his father can afford to

---

7. See Wendy Mayer, "Patronage, Pastoral Care and the Role of the Bishop at Antioch," *VC* 55, no. 1 (2001): 58–70.

8. See Frans van de Paverd, *St. John Chrysostom, The Homilies on the Statues: An Introduction* (Rome: Orientalium, 1991). The parallel is found at *Stag.* 1.3 (PG 47: 429.58–430.7) and *Stat.* 7.2 (PG 49: 94.7–18).

keep slaves, as well as his illegitimate children.[9] This is what would have afforded Stagirius a proper literate education. Not only is Stagirius apparently able to read Chrysostom's high-level Greek, but he also spends much of his time poring over the Scriptures in private.[10] Despite his father's licentiousness, Stagirius apparently belongs to a Christian family—or at least some of his family members are Christian and have raised him in the faith.[11] Whereas he used to live a life of ease,[12] he has taken up the life of a monk and pursues this calling with vigor.

Syrian Asceticism

What can be said with some certainty about John's early life is that before his presbyterate, John pursued some sort of ascetic regimen.[13] Socrates and Palladius relate as much, even if their accounts of John's early life are otherwise far from consistent. According to Socrates's account, John was trained in rhetoric and planned to work as a lawyer, but instead embraced the "quiet life," involving reading the Scriptures and frequenting church. He then "became [a disciple] of Diodore and Carterius in the ascetic life, who then presided over a monastic school (*asktētēria*)."[14] After this, John was ordained deacon by Meletius, one of the Nicene bishops in Antioch, and eventually retired to the solitary life: "John withdrew (*anachōreō*) and lived quietly for three whole years," before he was eventually ordained a priest.[15]

Palladius gives a rather different account of the chronology of John's life, but like Socrates he emphasizes John's monastic life prior to his ecclesiastical career:

---

9. *Stag.* 2.3 (PG 47: 452).
10. *Stag.* 1.10 (PG 47: 447); 2.1 (PG 47: 450).
11. *Stag.* 1.2 (PG 47: 427).
12. *Stag.* 1.10 (PG 47: 447).
13. Wendy Mayer, "What does it mean to say that John Chrysostom was a monk?" *StPatr* 41 (2006): 451–55.
14. Socrates, *Hist. eccl.* 6.3.
15. Ibid.

INTRODUCTION

But spurred on by his conscience, he could not be satisfied with the toil of the city ... he occupied the nearby mountains; here he fell in with an old Syrian man who practiced continence. He imitated his austerity, spending four years with him and contending with pleasure's storms. When he easily overcame these, not so much by toil as by reason, he withdrew alone to a cave, striving for obscurity, and there he spent twenty-four months. He remained most of the time sleepless, studying thoroughly the covenants of Christ, to banish his ignorance. And without reclining, night or day, for two years, he deadened his stomach organs, and from the cold the function of his kidneys was harmed. Since he wasn't any use to himself, he descended once again to the haven of the church.[16]

While Palladius's account of John's illness and return to the city clearly serves an apologetic purpose,[17] and it is unlikely that John lived as an ascetic for a full six years, his account is probably more accurate than that of Socrates. Not only does Palladius make fewer glaring mistakes, but he also seems to have been closely acquainted with John when the latter was Bishop of Constantinople. Furthermore, although some have thought that Palladius's account of asceticism is too "Egyptian" (Palladius having spent much time in Egypt and being the author of a famous monastic work, the *Lausiac History*),[18] his account of John's vigils and stasis[19] accord quite well with some distinctive characteristics of Syrian monasticism. So while we are left with a fair amount of uncertainty with respect to the early chronology of John's life and what his particular ascetic life entailed, it is quite clear that he benefited from an ascetic regimen in the environs of Antioch before he took up an active ecclesiastical career.

Palladius's quotation above reveals his—and probably also John's—familiarity with a particular form of Syrian asceticism, which is usually referred to as "extreme." While this is not a particularly descriptive term, it refers to some ascetic

16. Palladius, *Dial.* 5.
17. Mayer, "Making of a Saint."
18. This is a major contention in Martin Illert, *Johannes Chrysostomus und das antiochenische-syrische Mönchtum. Studien zu Theologie, Rhetorik und Kirchenpolitik im antiochenischen Schrifttum des Johannes Chrysostomus* (Zurich: Pano, 2000).
19. For definitions of these two terms, see the following paragraph.

practices that are distinctive to Syria at this time, and which seem not to have been widely practiced elsewhere. Prominent among these are sleep deprivation ("keeping vigil") and abstaining from sitting or reclining ("stasis"). I mention this because this particular form of ascetic life seems also to be echoed in John's account of Stagirius's life. At the beginning of the second book, Chrysostom relates that Stagirius's fellow ascetics are astounded—and even disturbed and concerned—at the extent of Stagirius's discipline. Chrysostom mentions his fasting—only water and bread—and not only vigils, but continuous sleepless nights. Stagirius also keeps continuous silence, makes a practice of crying, and reads Scripture continuously.[20] In Chrysostom's more famous work, *On the Priesthood*, when he has occasion to discuss the difference between the monk and the priest, he also describes such an "extreme" form of *askesis:* "intense fasting, sleeping on the ground, keeping vigil, going unwashed, much sweat, and everything else that they attend to for the humiliation of the body ..."[21] This extreme asceticism would come to its climax in the famous Stylites of the fifth century, whose lives the Antiochene Theodoret of Cyrrhus would record in his *Religious History*.[22] Whether Chrysostom had in fact personally undertaken such extreme discipline in his own life prior to his ordination to the priesthood remains an open question, since he could have learned of this way of life simply by making a habit of visiting the local monks—something that he often exhorted his flock to do.[23]

I have intentionally lapsed into describing the above forms of asceticism with the vague adjective "extreme," because there is also a less zealous ascetic counterpoint local to Antioch. Chrysostom describes this way of life in another of his ascetic works, *To Demetrius on Compunction*, which was probably

20. *Stag.* 1.10 (PG 47: 447); *Stag.* 2.1 (PG 47: 450).
21. *Sacer.* 6.5 (SC 272, 322).
22. The most famous being Simeon, on whom see Theodoret, *Hist. rel.* 26.
23. Samantha L. Miller, "Chrysostom's Monks as Living Exhortations to Poverty and the Rich Life," *GOTR* 58 (2013): 79–98. See, e.g., John Chrysostom, *Hom. Matt.* 69.3; *Hom. 1 Tim.* 14.3–6.

also written early in his ecclesiastical career. From this treatise we learn that his observation of the Syrian asceticism local to Antioch included the following:

When I left the city to go to the monks' abodes, I inquired much and investigated this: where the provision of necessities comes from, whether it is possible to eat fresh bread every day, whether someone will force me to use the same oil both for light and for food, whether someone will force me to the humiliation of eating pulses and throw me into difficult work—such as ordering me to dig, to carry wood or water, or to render service in various other ways.[24]

This form of asceticism obviously included elements common to various developing ascetic ways of life in late antiquity, especially the renunciation of much food and possessions. But it also indicates something that was common to Syrian asceticism, namely a sort of apprenticeship model of asceticism, which included significant manual labor.[25] Although in this region asceticism was often a solitary activity without any kind of coenobitic rule—even in an incipient form—disciples would often form a circle around a master. It is not entirely clear how this form of semi-communal asceticism relates to Stagirius's situation. We do hear some hints of a community: there are monks who sleep near Stagirius. Chrysostom also received news of Stagirius from someone close to the monk: a certain Theophilus the Ephesian.[26] How such communities might have related to the "school"—the *askētērion*—of Diodore and Carterius is an open question.[27] Whatever the case,

---

24. *Demetr.* 6 (PG 47: 403).
25. See Columba Stewart, "The Ascetic Taxonomy of Antioch and Edessa at the Emergence of Monasticism," *Adamantius* 19 (2013): 207–21; Joseph Patrich, *Sabas, Leader of Palestinian Monasticism: A Comparative Study in Eastern Monasticism, Fourth to Seventh Centuries* (Washington, DC: Dumbarton Oaks, 1995), 22–28.
26. *Stag.* 1.1.
27. See Robert G. T. Edwards, "Grammar in the School of Diodore of Tarsus: An Institutional Context for the Transfer of Exegetical Knowledge," in *Knowledge Construction in Late Antiquity*, ed. Monika Amsler (Berlin: De Gruyter, 2023), 257–81. There were certainly other forms of monasticism in the area at this time. See Elizabeth A. Clark, "John Chrysostom and the 'Subintroductae,'" *CH* 46, no. 2 (1977): 171–85; Blake Leyerle, *Theatrical Shows and Ascetic Lives: John Chrysostom's Attack on Spiritual Marriage* (Berkeley: University of California Press,

Chrysostom was in some way familiar with these various forms of monastic life, and was personally connected to these communities, such that he was put in touch with Stagirius himself.

Despondency, Consolation, and Ancient Medicine

When Chrysostom learns of Stagirius's illness from their mutual friend, Theophilus the Ephesian, he is dismayed to hear the extent of Stagirius's condition. The illness is described in some detail, even if not from a first-hand account.[28] His physical symptoms are described by Chrysostom in a distressing manner: "the writhing of the hands, the rolling of the eyes, the froth from the mouth, that ill-omened and obscure voice, the shaking of the body, the prolonged unconsciousness, and the dream that appeared that night."[29] Various scholars have observed that what Chrysostom here describes is likely epilepsy, though, as Ulrich Volp noticed, Chrysostom himself never makes such a diagnosis because of the social stigma associated with it.[30] Whatever the retro-diagnosis, Chrysostom takes little interest in the diagnosis and treatment of this illness.

Instead, Chrysostom is concerned with the *spiritual* aetiology and the *spiritual* consequences of the "falling sickness." Such a concern is not surprising given that Stagirius ails from things other than these seizures. He is also suicidal, to the point of being drawn to cliff tops, the riverside, and the seaside.[31] We have already heard that he is plagued by terrors in the night.

2001); Wendy Mayer, "Monasticism at Antioch and Constantinople in the Late Fourth Century: A Case of Exclusivity or Diversity?" in *Prayer and Spirituality in the Early Church*, ed. Pauline Allen, Raymond Canning, Lawrence Cross, and Janelle B. Caiger (Everton Park, Qld., Australia: Centre for Early Christian Studies, Australian Catholic University, 1998).

28. It is not even clear that Theophilus himself witnessed one of Stagirius's fits, or whether he had only heard about them.

29. *Stag.* 1.1 (PG 47: 426).

30. Ulrich Volp, "'That Unclean Spirit Has Assaulted You from the Very Beginning': John Chrysostom and Suicide," *StPatr* 47 (2010): 273–86.

31. *Stag.* 1.1 (PG 47: 425–426). Also see *Stag.* 2.1 (PG 47: 447).

According to the report of a monastic whose quarters are near those of Stagirius, he is seized by "the demon"—that is, he has a fit—as a result of these dreams.[32] Much more, however, than all of these symptoms, which may be associated with the work of a demon, Chrysostom's real worry is Stagirius's emotional sickness: his despondency (*athumia*).[33] In fact, instead of making the danger of demon-harassment the theme of his whole work (as the common Byzantine title would indicate), he instead makes *athumia* the theme, especially of Books 2 and 3. It is therefore this sickness of the soul, rather than a sickness of the body, that Chrysostom works to diagnose and to treat.

When it comes to identifying the cause of *athumia*, several candidates arise throughout the treatise. One explanation for the cause of *athumia* is an excess. The problem is not simply that Stagirius is experiencing *athumia*, since when *athumia* is not excessive it is capable of being put to good use: namely, grieving over one's sins, which will lead to repentance.[34] Instead—according to this reading—the problem is that Stagirius has an excess (*hyperbolē*) of *athumia*, which in turn causes the other symptoms associated with the demon.[35] This explanation is in part based on a humoral medical model, which Chrysostom does seem to be aware of. Although Chrysostom is careful *not* to refer to Stagirius's illness as *melancholia*—itself characterized in ancient medical literature as an excess of black bile—Chrysostom's use of the language of excess points in this direction.

A medical explanation, however, for *athumia* coming from humoral excess is less prominent in the *Consolation to Stagirius* than the explanation that the *athumia* stems from Stagirius's faulty judgments (*logismoi*). Even if Stagirius's *logismoi* are not yet grievously faulty, they appear to be dangerously close to

---

32. *Stag.* 1.1 (PG 47: 426).
33. See, especially, *Stag.* 2.1 (PG 47: 447–448). On *athumia* in *Ad Stagirium*, see M.-A Bardolle, "Tristesse (*athumia*) et thérapeutique spirituelle dans l'*Exhortation à Stagire* de Chrysostome," *Lettre de Ligugé* 241, no. 3 (1987): 6–19.
34. *Stag.* 3.14 (PG 47: 491–492).
35. Blake Leyerle, "The Etiology of Sorrow and its Therapeutic Benefits in the Preaching of John Chrysostom," *JLA* 8, no. 2 (2015): 368–85. Leyerle also points to his excessive ascetic habits.

the point of making Stagirius fall away. What is the content of Stagirius's incorrect judgments? It has been suggested that Stagirius is too concerned with his own reputation (*doxa*). He considers his good reputation to be of true value, and in light of this value judgment, his seizures are causing him to sink into despondency. Having left behind the unfortunate and disreputable situation of his adulterous father, whose mistresses had borne him many illegitimate children, Stagirius has renounced this life only to find that he is now being embarrassed by a shameful illness in the company of his fellow monastics.[36] This is clear enough in the treatise. That Stagirius, however, judges his reputation to be a good instead of what it really is—indifferent—is connected to a more significant problematic judgment: Stagirius does not trust in the goodness of God's providence—or at least he does not trust in it sufficiently. Though I will say more about divine providence momentarily, for now it will suffice to say that Stagirius's *logismoi* are faulty insofar as he calls into question the goodness of divine providence, by questioning the benefit that might come from the illness—since it has been providentially given to Stagirius for his training (*paideia*).[37] We can see throughout Chrysostom's works that questioning divine providence is a dangerous spiritual problem, one for which he will at times even condemn the heretics.[38]

As I have already noted, however, *athumia* is not all negative. For the most part, Chrysostom understands that emotions can be employed both positively and negatively. Chrysostom thus makes every effort in his sermons to provoke appropriate emotional responses from his audience.[39] Accordingly, Chrysostom

---

36. Jessica Wright, "Between Despondency and the Demon: Diagnosing and Treating Spiritual Disorders in John Chrysostom's *Letter to Stageirios*," *JLA* 8, no. 2 (2015): 352–67.

37. See *Stag.* 1.1 (PG 47: 426).

38. See especially *Anom.* [*De incomp.*] 2. See Robert G. T. Edwards, "Divine Incomprehensibility and Human Faith in John Chrysostom," *VC* 76, no. 4 (2022): 434–62.

39. See Blake Leyerle, *The Narrative Shape of Emotion in the Preaching of John Chrysostom* (Berkeley: University of California Press, 2020); eadem, "The Strategic Use of Fear in the Preaching of John Chrysostom," in *Social Control in Late*

presents *athumia* as not only an illness (in its excess), but also as a course of medical treatment. Despondency is entirely appropriate in the case of those who have sinned grievously and require repentance. But *athumia* can also appear in a neutral sense. In Books 2 and 3 especially, Chrysostom demonstrates that, even if *athumia* is not done away with, it can be endured. Throughout these books, all the righteous—the patriarchs, the prophets, and the apostle Paul—have suffered difficult external circumstances along with the *athumia* that so often accompanies these experiences. Yet none of these men stumbled, none were disturbed, and all held fast to God's goodness, love for humanity, and providence. These saints desponded, but not excessively, and utilized correct judgments (*logismoi*) as a help and a therapy.

The *Consolation to Stagirius* is thus—as the English title indicates—a consolatory work. It works to reduce the recipient's *athumia* and to offer arguments that will lead instead to *euthumia*, joy. But can these three books therefore be called a "consolation" in the classical sense? Some have answered in the negative because the work is not *only* consolatory but also hortatory. In addition to the long and unconventional literary form of the work, it cannot be said to fit comfortably within the classical genre of consolation, which included mostly letters and funeral encomia. Nevertheless, if we consider the social function of consolations,[40] then this work certainly fits within the confines of the classical and particularly the late antique consolatory tradition. Consolations were rarely concerned *merely* to console the bereaved, but they were also used as opportunities to discern a new way forward in the face of tragic loss. It is also worth noting that while Chrysostom em-

---

Antiquity: The Violence of Small Worlds, ed. Kate Cooper and Jamie Wood (Cambridge: Cambridge University Press, 2020), 173–87; eadem, "Etiology of Sorrow."

40. As suggested by J. H. D. Scourfield, "Towards a Genre of Consolation," in *Greek and Roman Consolations: Eight Studies of a Tradition and its Afterlife,* ed. Han Baltussen (Swansea: Classical Press of Wales, 2013), 1–36; also see, in the same volume, Han Baltussen, "Introduction," in *Greek and Roman Consolations: Eight Studies of a Tradition and its Afterlife,* ed. Han Baltussen (Swansea: Classical Press of Wales, 2013), xiii–xx.

phasizes at the beginning of the *Consolation to Stagirius* that the work is "consolatory," he was a writer and speaker who rarely felt bound by the constraints of genre. It is for this reason that scholars have struggled to classify many of his works.[41] What Chrysostom provides in the *Consolation to Stagirius* is thus his own way of consolation.[42]

As consolatory literature, *To Stagirius* is also therapeutic. There is a growing awareness that literature such as this does more than simply make someone feel better, in a modern, western sense. Instead, therapeutic works like the *Consolation to Stagirius* seek to reorient one's underlying, foundational value judgments, under the conviction that such rational judgments will lead one to healthier emotions—which are themselves also rational.[43] Chrysostom thus seeks in this treatise to replace Stagirius's faulty set of assumptions—about what

---

41. See, for example, the question of the genre of *Ad eos qui scandalizati sunt*: Margaret A. Schatkin, *John Chrysostom as Apologist: With Special Reference to De incomprehensibili, Quod nemo laeditur, Ad eos qui scandalizati sunt, and Adversus oppugnatores vitae monasticae* (Thessaloniki: Patriarchikon Hidryma Paterikōn Meletōn, 1987), 107–9. Also, the *De laudibus Pauli* are not quite encomia: Margaret M. Mitchell, *The Heavenly Trumpet: John Chrysostom and the Art of Pauline Interpretation* (Tübingen: Mohr Siebeck, 2000), 378–79, following Harry M. Hubbell, "Chrysostom and Rhetoric," *CP* 19, no. 3 (1924): 268; and his homilies are not quite diatribes: Arnold Uleyn, "La doctrine morale de saint Jean Chrysostome dans le Commentaire sur saint Matthieu et ses affinités avec la diatribe," *Revue de l'Université d'Ottawa* 27, no. 1–2 (1957): 25.

42. Chrysostom's way of consolation can fruitfully be compared with that of the Cappadocian fathers; Robert G. T. Edwards, *Providence and Narrative in the Theology of John Chrysostom* (Cambridge: Cambridge University Press, 2022), 149–53. On the Cappadocian fathers and consolation, see Robert C. Gregg, *Consolation Philosophy: Greek and Christian Paideia in Basil and the Two Gregories* (Cambridge, MA: Philadelphia Patristic Foundation, 1975).

43. Christopher Gill has been at the forefront of demonstrating this in Greco-Roman antiquity more broadly; see Christopher Gill, "Philosophical Therapy as Preventative Psychological Medicine," in *Mental Disorders in the Classical World*, ed. William V. Harris (Leiden: Brill, 2013), 339–60; and his earlier essay, "Ancient Psychotherapy," *Journal of the History of Ideas* 46, no. 3 (1985): 307–25. Wendy Mayer has been responsible for bringing this insight to bear in the work of John Chrysostom; see Wendy Mayer, "Shaping the Sick Soul: Reshaping the Identity of John Chrysostom," in *Christians Shaping Identity from the Roman Empire to Byzantium: Studies Inspired by Pauline Allen*, ed. Geoffrey Dunn and Wendy Mayer (Leiden: Brill, 2015), 143–45; Wendy Mayer, "The Persistence in Late Antiquity of Medico-Philosophical Psychic Therapy," *JLA* 8, no. 2 (2015): 337–51.

has value and what does not, about what is a good and what is not—with respect both to rational arguments and, especially, to demonstrations from Scripture. These faulty foundational judgments are the *logismoi* that we have already identified as the causes of Stagirius's ailment: that reputation is a good, and that affliction—which is in fact from God—is not.

Divine Providence, Philanthropy, and Human Suffering

The central true judgment with which Chrysostom seeks to console Stagirius throughout all three books is that affliction is providentially given by God and that it has a positive end: salvation and good repute. The corollary is that the only true evil (*kakia*) in the world comes from the human will—that is, from the sin of individuals.[44] Thus suffering, or, as John often terms it, affliction (*thlipsis*), is neither evil nor indifferent, but manifestly positive, because it is given by God and because it is providentially directed towards the end of the salvation of human beings.[45] Chrysostom's primary means of demonstrating the goodness of affliction is with reference to the saints of Scripture who have suffered more than anyone, and yet have continued to trust in and be directed by God's providence.

"Providence" is a significant theological term found all throughout Chrysostom's works.[46] It is his chief way of referring

---

44. This argument is also especially prevalent in *De diabolo tentatore* (esp. hom. 1) and in the later treatises and letters, *Quod nemo laeditur nisi a se ipso*, *Ad eos qui scandalizati sunt*, and the *Letters to Olympias*.

45. See Robert G. T. Edwards, "Providence, Ethics, and Exempla: Reassessing the Stoicism of John Chrysostom's *Quod nemo laeditur nisi a se ipso*," in *Greek and Byzantine Philosophical Exegesis*, ed. J. B. Wallace and A. Despotis (Paderborn: Schöningh, 2022), 217–43, against the previous consensus in, e.g., Emmanuel Amand de Mendieta, "L'amplification d'un thème socratique et stoïcien dans l'avant dernier traité de Jean Chrysostome," *Byzantion* 36 (1966): 353–81; Edward Nowak, *Le chrétien devant la souffrance. Étude sur la pensée de Jean Chrysostome* (Paris: Beauchesne, 1972).

46. Most recent is Edwards, *Providence and Narrative in the Theology of John Chrysostom* (full reference in note 42 above). Earlier treatments include George D. Dragas, "St. John Chrysostom's Doctrine of God's Providence," *Ekklesiastikos Pharos* 57 (1957): 375–406; Christopher A. Hall, "Nature Wild and Tame in St.

to divine activity and is thus a massive category. As for many other thinkers in late antiquity, Christian and otherwise, it was for Chrysostom a general term denoting the divine ordering of the cosmos, the nations, individual human beings, and—for Christians—the Church.[47] Although Chrysostom never sets out to define providence, a rough contemporary of his from Syria, Nemesius of Emesa, did: "Providence, then, is care for things by God. It is also defined as follows: providence is the wish of God by which all things receive a suitable way of life."[48] Without actually defining providence, Chrysostom would appear to share the basic content of Nemesius's definition as, in another of Chrysostom's treatises on providence, he writes, "[God] is the beginning and the cause and the source of all goods; he is the Creator, he brought forward the things that did not exist; and he supports, regulates, and maintains that which he brought forward, as he wishes."[49]

Although many ancient thinkers engaged the question of

John Chrysostom's On the Providence of God," in *Ancient and Postmodern Christianity: Paleo-Orthodoxy in the 21st Century: Essays in Honor of Thomas C. Oden,* ed. Kenneth Tanner and Christopher A. Hall (Downers Grove, IL: InterVarsity, 2002), 23–37; Theresia Hainthaler, "*Pronoia* bei Johannes Chrysostomus in *De providentia* und seinen Briefen an Olympias," in *Pronoia. The Providence of God. Die Vorsehung Gottes. Forscher aus dem Osten und Westen Europas an den Quellen des gemeinsamen Glauben: Studientagung Warschau, 30. August–4. September 2017,* ed. T. Hainthaler, F. Mali, and M. Lenkaityte Ostermann (Innsbruck: Tyrolia, 2019), 145–61.

47. For an overview of ancient philosophical perspectives, see Myrto Dragona-Monachou, "Divine Providence in the Philosophy of Empire," *ANRW* II 36, no. 7 (1994): 4417–90; Albrecht Dihle, "Liberté et destin dans l'antiquité tardive," *Revue de Théologie et de Philosophie* 121 (1989): 129–47. On Stoicism in particular, see Keimpe Algra, "Stoic Theology," in *The Cambridge Companion to the Stoics,* ed. Brad Inwood (Cambridge: Cambridge University Press, 2006), 153–78; Thomas Bénatouïl, "How Industrious can Zeus be?" in *God and Cosmos in Stoicism,* ed. Ricardo Salles (Oxford: Oxford University Press, 2009), 23–45.

48. *Hom. nat.* 42 (Teubner, 125), trans. R. W. Sharples and Philip Van der Eijk, *Nemesius: On the Nature of Man* (Liverpool: Liverpool University Press, 2008), 208. On Nemesius of Emesa's reflection on a Christian doctrine of providence and its alternatives, see R. W. Sharples, "Nemesius of Emesa and Some Theories of Divine Providence," *VC* 37, no. 2 (1983): 141–56; R. W. Sharples, "Threefold Providence: The History and Background of a Doctrine," *Bulletin of the Institute of Classical Studies. Supplement, 78: Ancient Approaches to Plato's Timaeus* (2003): 107–27.

49. *Scand.* 2.9 (SC 79, 64).

the providence that governs the cosmos and human beings in particular—including prominent Christian philosophers such as Clement of Alexandria, Origen, Gregory of Nyssa, and Maximus Confessor[50]—Chrysostom's own use of the idea fits nicely into an Antiochene Christian context in which providence was frequently discussed. Diodore of Tarsus, one of Chrysostom's teachers of exegesis and theology, wrote a now-lost treatise *On Providence,* Theodoret of Cyrrhus likewise wrote ten orations *On Providence,* and Nemesius of Emesa discusses these topics at length at the end of his *De natura hominis.* Chrysostom's own final treatise (*To Those who have Fallen*) has sometimes been entitled *On the Providence of God;* and the *Consolation to Stagirius* was even published in the early modern period under the title *Three Books on the Providence of God.*[51]

Philosophical discussions of providence—especially informed by Stoicism—were often highly anthropocentric. They concerned not only how God cared for the cosmos generally, but especially how God ordered things for the benefit of humankind. Chrysostom's vision is also anthropocentric, but this is especially because he comes to his understanding of God's care for humankind through his reading of Scripture. Throughout his works, and in the *Consolation to Stagirius* itself, providence is said to be directed to the end of human salvation: "Even if we sin ten thousand times, and even if we turn from him, he does not cease to arrange what is for our salva-

---

50. There is no general survey of early Christian teaching on providence. For introductions to the topic, see Silke-Petra Bergjan, *Der fürsorgende Gott: Der Begriff der ΠΡΟΝΟΙΑ Gottes in der apologetischen Literatur der Alten Kirche* (Berlin: De Gruyter, 2002); Andrew Louth, "Pagans and Christians on Providence," in *Text and Culture in Late Antiquity: Inheritance, Authority and Change,* ed. J. H. D. Scourfield and Anna Chahoud (Swansea: Classical Press of Wales, 2007), 279–97; Ken Parry, "Fate, Free Choice, and Divine Providence from the Neoplatonists to John of Damascus," in *The Cambridge Intellectual History of Byzantium,* ed. Anthony Kaldellis and Niketas Siniossoglou (Cambridge: Cambridge University Press, 2017), 341–60; Bronwen Neil, "Divine Providence and Free Will in Gregory of Nyssa and His Theological Milieu," *Phronema* 27, no. 2 (2012): 35–51.

51. Jean-Noël Guinot, "Les *exempla* bibliques dans l'*Ad Stagirium* de Jean Chrysostome: Proposition d'une clef de lecture," in *Giovanni Crisostomo: Oriente e occidente tra IV e V secolo, XXXIII Incontro di Studiosi dell'Antichità Cristiana, Roma, 6–8 Maggio 2004* (Rome: Augustinianum, 2005), 170, note 26.

tion, so that we may turn again and be saved."[52] Chrysostom arrives at this view through his interpretation of biblical narratives—those he focuses on throughout the *Consolation to Stagirius*—and also through his central convictions concerning God's *philanthrōpia* (love for humanity) and *sunkatabasis* (condescension or adaptability).[53] The former is especially important for Chrysostom, because it explains *sunkatabasis,* and indeed is logically prior to it: God adapts himself (condescends) to humanity's weakness and limitations precisely because he has such great love and affection for his human creatures. In the same way, *philanthrōpia* is logically prior to providence inasmuch as God's arrangement of the cosmos is ordered to the end of the good of humanity. This good end is variously articulated by Chrysostom as humanity's good repute, honor, and salvation. In another treatise, he writes, "The economy looks to one end ...: our salvation and good repute."[54]

Also important for Chrysostom is the distinction between what is up to God's providence and what is up to us or in our power. This is the distinction between actions or events that are God's responsibility and those that are the responsibility of individual human beings, and it was a longstanding distinction in ancient philosophical discussions. Although the distinction did not begin with the Stoics, they are the ones who popularized it; and by Chrysostom's time, virtually all philosophical schools made sense of this distinction in various ways—at least, every school that held to the idea that some divine providence does in fact oversee the cosmos. For Chrysostom, this distinction means that all "externals" (what is not up to us) are up to providence. This implies that there is no external evil, with evil residing only in the human will (*prohairesis*) or mindset (*gnōmē*).[55] Such thinking leads

---

52. *Stag.* 1.2 (PG 47: 428). Also see *Stag.* 1.5 (PG 47: 437): "For each day many great things are ordered for our salvation."

53. On the topic of *sunkatabasis*, see David Rylaarsdam, *John Chrysostom on Divine Pedagogy: The Coherence of his Theology and Preaching* (Oxford: Oxford University Press, 2014).

54. *Scand.* 9.5 (SC 79, 146).

55. On which, see Raymond Laird, *Mindset, Moral Choice and Sin in the Anthropology of John Chrysostom* (Strathfield, NSW, Australia: St Pauls, 2012).

Chrysostom to the claim that Satan, being limited only to persuasion and not coercion, has no power over human responsibility and is therefore in no respect to blame for evil.[56]

This distinction between human and divine activity leads Chrysostom to what takes up much of the discussion and exegesis throughout the treatise: the benefit of suffering.[57] Chrysostom naturally has an abundance of Scriptures to muster in favor of such an argument. But the benefit of suffering also follows logically from what we have already heard: if externals are providentially ordered towards humanity's good, so even suffering—even the *greatest* suffering—must be embraced as the work of God's providence. Even if human beings (even Chrysostom himself) habitually refer to suffering as evil, this suffering is not *properly* called evil.[58] Therefore, suffering is not indifferent, as the Stoics hold, but a manifest good. And what sort of benefits does it bring about? Chrysostom recognizes the pastoral difficulty with introducing such a topic, and so is careful not to claim that Stagirius's suffering is punishment for sins—though it certainly can happen that suffering serves as chastisement for sins and therefore an impetus to moral improvement. Rather, as we learn at the end of the treatise, suffering is instrumental for leading to repentance, trust in, and discourse with God.[59]

Biblical Interpretation

Whereas Chrysostom does demonstrate the benefits of suffering philosophically, through rational arguments (*logismoi*), he more often exhibits them by relating biblical narratives. These narratives exhibit various truths, but primarily they show how righteous men have suffered—including suffering

---

56. *Stag.* 1.4 (PG 47: 434).
57. On suffering in John Chrysostom, see Nowak, *Chrétien devant la souffrance;* Douglas Finn, "Sympathetic Philosophy: The Christian Response to Suffering according to John Chrysostom's Commentary on Job," in *Suffering and Evil in Early Christian Thought,* ed. Nonna Verna Harrison and David G. Hunter (Grand Rapids, MI: Baker Academic, 2016), 97–119.
58. See *Diab.* 1.
59. *Stag.* 3.14 (PG 47: 492–493).

from *athumia*—and yet have continued to live righteously and to be cared for providentially. This is the primary mode of biblical interpretation in the *Consolation to Stagirius*, especially in Book 1. Furthermore, scriptural exempla are brought to bear in Chrysostom's demonstration that God is providential *both* in those events that are obviously good and in those that are apparently evil. Thus creation (Gn 1-2) is obviously a good: many generous gifts are given to Adam and Eve. At the same time, the punishment that comes after the sin of the same pair (Gn 3), although it seems to be an evil, is in fact a good—no less than creation is itself. All that Adam and Eve receive as punishment is "toil and sweat"—a small price to pay for spitting on God's goodness and disobeying him. Furthermore, death is itself a mercy, since the alternative would be for Adam and Eve to continue sinning forever.[60] Chrysostom thus carefully interprets all the minute details of the narrative to demonstrate that within the same narrative, events that seem to be opposed to one another—those that are truly good and those that are apparently bad—are in fact in agreement, insofar as they share in the same divine love and providence. This is the thrust of the biblical interpretation that dominates Book 1.

In Books 2 and 3, the biblical interpretation takes a turn. Whereas Chrysostom continues to rely on biblical narratives, particularly from the Old Testament, they serve a different purpose. They are less immediately concerned with divine providence and are instead adduced to demonstrate how many of the righteous whose lives are narrated in Scripture have suffered not only from all forms of external affliction, but also, like Stagirius himself, from *athumia*—despondency. Chrysostom goes on at length to prove this is the case for all those from Genesis and Exodus to Joshua and the prophets,

---

60. *Stag.* 1.3 (PG 47: 429). On Chrysostom's interpretations of the creation accounts in Genesis, see Catherine Broc-Schmezer, "Lectures et récritures chrysostomiennes des premiers chapitres de la Genèse," *Graphè* 17 (2008): 95–125; Cyrille Crépey, "Le vrai sens de la littéralité de l'exégèse dans les Homélies sur la Genèse de Jean Chrysostome: illustration à partir de l'exégèse de Gn 1:1," *StPatr* 47 (2010): 249–54.

to David and Paul. Why does he do this? It is at least in part to make clear to Stagirius that his suffering is nothing compared to that of the patriarchs or prophets (and Chrysostom even includes two figures, real or imagined, from his own day).[61] But it is also to show that God does indeed allow even those most favored by him—that is, the righteous—to suffer grievously, and that this presents no challenge to the idea that God does love and favor them. Furthermore, it is important to Chrysostom that Stagirius identify with these individuals. Chrysostom is very clear that Stagirius, who is so virtuous, is among the number of the righteous.

Chrysostom uses several tactics to highlight these figures' sufferings, and to have Stagirius closely identify with them in their suffering. First, as also in his interpretations in Book 1, he draws out every small narrative detail to show the suffering of the individual. For example, despite the silence of the biblical text as to Abraham's emotions, Chrysostom shows how "likely" (*eikos*) it is that he suffered and desponded—because anyone in such a situation would have suffered. Chrysostom creates an immediacy to this and other situations of profound suffering, striking a deeply personal and highly emotional note. Having narrated Abraham's near-sacrifice of Isaac, he reaches a rhetorical climax:

When Abraham was ordered to sacrifice and burn up with his own hands his legitimate and firstborn son, who was born to him against hope, after so much time, in extreme old age (for these things excite an even greater flame), who was still young, did Abraham suffer nothing human? What could be more ridiculous than saying this? For if he were made of stone, iron, or adamant itself, wouldn't he be bent and broken because of the age of his son (for he was still in the bloom of youth), because of the significance of his words, and because of the piety of his soul?[62]

Thus, using a wide variety of rhetorical techniques, Chrysostom presents the suffering of Abraham and other biblical charac-

---

61. One, Aristoxenus the Bithynian (*Stag.* 3.12; PG 47: 489), and another, Demophilus (*Stag.* 3.12; PG 47: 489), both now unknown to us—unless they are fictional.
62. *Stag.* 2.9 (PG 47: 462).

ters before Stagirius's eyes.[63] Thus in many instances, as he interprets the narratives of Abraham and other biblical figures, Chrysostom puts in the hard work of interpreting biblical narratives, helping Stagirius to enter into the reality of the characters' sufferings.

In other cases, Chrysostom has Stagirius put in the hard work himself. For while at times Chrysostom offers up every little detail, at other times he is very allusive. Time and again he tells Stagirius that he is omitting all kinds of other sufferings that biblical figures went through, and thus makes Stagirius work to remember them for himself. For example, having already gone through many of Noah's sufferings, he writes, "I pass over the multitude of beasts and creeping things with whom he was yoked together for so long while he was enclosed in such a small space,"[64] thus having Stagirius imagine the situation for himself. Chrysostom later notes that, as Moses did in his narration of Abraham's life, he too will omit details about Abraham's life before God speaks to him to "go" in Genesis 12.[65] He thus stimulates Stagirius's imagination, including perhaps popular accounts of Abraham's early life that find their way into various midrashic and apocryphal narratives.

Later in his narration of Abraham's life, Chrysostom "pass[es] over the quarrel between the shepherds and the distribution of land to his nephew. If we were to scrutinize these events at another time, they would be sufficient to cast one into much despondency."[66] This is a slightly different tactic because it requires less that Stagirius use his imagination and more that he use his memory: what was it that happened between Abraham and Lot and the shepherds who worked for them? Likewise with the story of Moses:

But having heard these difficulties, don't think that it was only these things that happened. In fact, I have omitted not a few of the things that occurred: battles, opposition from enemies, long jour-

---

63. On this kind of "engaged exegesis," see Judit Kecskeméti, "Exégèse Chrysostomienne et exégèse engagée," *StPatr* 22 (1989): 136–47.
64. *Stag.* 2.5 (PG 47: 455).
65. *Stag.* 2.6 (PG 47: 457).
66. *Stag.* 2.7 (PG 47: 460).

neys, and his sister's offense, at whose punishment that gentlest man Moses was distressed even more. But nevertheless, even if someone should precisely add everything up, what has been written is not one ten-thousandth part of what happened.[67]

One final example of the phenomenon of having Stagirius recall sufferings narrated in Scripture is Chrysostom's extremely allusive comment: "This reminds me of the one who spent thirty-eight years in this suffering!"[68] This is an allusion to the paralyzed man who lay by the Pool of Bethesda, but whom Jesus healed (Jn 5.1–15). While I have no reason to doubt that Stagirius was learned in the Scriptures, it would probably take him some effort to recall the person who, in Scripture, is supposed to have suffered for this specific length of time. Through all this allusiveness, Chrysostom makes Stagirius exert himself in recalling these narratives of the righteous who have suffered and nevertheless believed in God and yielded to his good providence. And through this effort—whether of the imagination or of the memory—Stagirius "actualizes" these narratives and thus immerses himself in them, such that his soul might emulate the souls of those righteous men.

If I have so far said nothing about Chrysostom's "Antiochene" biblical interpretation, that is only because in the *Consolation to Stagirius* there is little evidence for it. Apart from the question of whether Chrysostom's exegetical method is in fact Antiochene,[69] there are hints here and there of interpre-

---

67. *Stag.* 3.4 (PG 47: 477).
68. *Stag.* 3.12 (PG 47: 489).
69. The now-classic treatment of Antiochene exegesis, which largely excludes John Chrysostom from the analysis, is Christoph Schäublin, *Untersuchungen zu Methode und Herkunft der antiochenischen Exegese* (Cologne: Hanstein, 1974). He is, however, included in the study of Robert C. Hill, *Reading the Old Testament in Antioch* (Leiden: Brill, 2005). For the question of whether Chrysostom should be regarded as an Antiochene exegete, see Robert G. T. Edwards, "The Gospel of John and Antiochene Christology: The Diverging Cases of Theodore of Mopsuestia and John Chrysostom," *SJT* 74, no. 4 (2021): 333–45. For an alternative way of considering the school of Antioch, in terms of common interpretations rather than a common *method* of interpretation, see Hagit Amirav, *Rhetoric and Tradition: John Chrysostom on Noah and the Flood* (Leuven: Peeters, 2003).

tations that the preacher could have picked up from his Antiochene context. The clearest example of Chrysostom's debt to an Antiochene tradition of exegesis is his interpretation of Adam's bearing the "image of God" (Gn 1.26) in Book 1. To bear this "image" is to hold a position relative to the rest of creation that is analogous to God's position over humankind: bearing "the image" is to have dominion over the earth similar to God's dominion over all of creation.[70] Thus, while the *Consolation to Stagirius* does provide some evidence of Chrysostom's place within an Antiochene interpretative tradition, Chrysostom's exegesis is more than mere Antiochenism.[71]

Notes on the Translation and Text

There are a few key terms that I have attempted to translate as consistently as possible. First, I always translate *athumia* as "despondency" and *athumeō* as "to despond." It is perhaps a little old-fashioned, but, as one of the few technical terms, it helps to see it clearly in the translation. Likewise, I always translate *euthumia* as "joy." Although there are other words with a *thum-* root—*thumos, epithumia,* and *prothumia*—these are not consistently translated with a single term; however, I have indicated in the footnotes when these terms occur.[72] Similarly, *pronoia* is always translated as "providence," but *kēdemonia*

---

70. Robert E. Carter, "The Image of God in Man and Woman according to Severian of Gabala and the Antiochene Tradition," *OCP* 69, no. 1 (2003): 163–78; Pak-Wah Lai, "The *Imago Dei* and Salvation among the Antiochenes: A Comparison of John Chrysostom with Theodore of Mopsuestia," *StPatr* 67 (2013): 393–402.

71. It is notable too that even some of those aspects that are often associated with John Chrysostom's exegesis are missing in this treatise, as also in his other early ascetic treatises, such as the idea of *akribeia* and, especially, *sunkatabasis*. See Robert C. Hill, "On Looking Again at *Sunkatabasis*," *Prudentia* 13 (1981): 3–11; idem, "*Akribeia*: A Principle of Chrysostom's Exegesis," *Colloquium* 14, no. 1 (1981): 32–36.

72. On this "play on words," see Laurence Brottier, "Un jeu de mots intraduisible: Le combat entre *thumos* et *athumia* dans des homélies de Jean Chrysostome," *Revue de Philologie, de Littérature et d'Histoire Anciennes* 72, no. 2 (1998): 189–204.

is alternatively translated as "care" and "providential care." I have not been so consistent with *philanthrōpia* and its cognates: sometimes this is "love for humankind" and sometimes simply "love." As with the *thum-* words, I have also indicated in the footnotes where other terms that I consider important occur. Furthermore, whereas I usually choose a specific term to render any given Greek term without any commentary, I do occasionally note an alternative sense of Greek terms that are especially ambiguous, especially where they bear on medical discourse.

Another central term in the treatise that requires some discussion is *daimonaō*. Although we might colloquially translate this into English as "demon-possessed," I have decided instead to translate it as "harassed by the/a demon." I translate it this way because the verb itself has no indication of "possession," and could be rendered in English with a more direct verb like "to demonize." This, however, obviously does not have the correct sense, and therefore an English translation requires another verb. "Harass" is preferable to "possess" because, as Chrysostom makes very clear throughout the treatise, the demon—like any demon—has *very little power* over Stagirius. It can touch the body, yes, but not the soul or the will. It cannot coerce. It can only persuade. Therefore, "harass" appropriately conveys the *external* nature of demonic activity.

I should also note that it is not only the content of the treatise that is allusive (as I mentioned above), but also the style. In contrast with much of Chrysostom's preaching, where the style is rather direct, in this more literary treatise Chrysostom communicates less directly. The subject or the object of any given sentence is not always clear, and the reader is left to infer what the writer might mean. In my translation, for the sake of ease of reading, I have chosen to supply the referent. Furthermore, where Chrysostom frequently makes use of near and far demonstrative pronouns, I found rendering these pronouns directly ("the former, the latter" or "this man, that man") very awkward, and so, again, I have most often supplied the direct referent. Even in these cases, I have been forced at many points to make inferences as to the referent of the demonstratives, some of which are more obvious than others. I have again, however, erred on the side of the clarity of the translation rather than having the reader of the translation stumble over awkward English constructions.

The Greek text translated comes from Migne's Patrologia Graeca. (The numbers throughout the translation refer to the column numbers of Volume 47 of that series.) While not a critical edition, it does make use of several earlier editions from the seventeenth and eighteenth centuries, namely those of Henry Savile, Fronton du Duc, and Bernard de Montfaucon. Although all of these early editions apparently relied on different manuscripts, the texts are remarkably similar. While the PG edition evidently took into account an additional manuscript, it mostly follows Montfaucon's "Benedictine Edition," but occasionally prefers readings from Savile.[73] I have translated almost exclusively the main text rather than the textual variants. On occasion, however, I note where a textual variant results in a significantly different reading.

[73]. On the editions of Savile and Duc, see Sam Kennerley, *The Reception of John Chrysostom in Early Modern Europe: Translating and Reading a Greek Father from 1417 to 1624* (Berlin: De Gruyter, 2023), 266–77.

CONSOLATION
TO STAGIRIUS

BOOK I

*John Chrysostom's Consolation to Stagirius,
a monk harassed by a demon*

IT WAS necessary for me, most beloved Stagirius, to be present with you now and to endure hardship together with you, exhorting with a (424) word, serving with an action, and, in brief, helping in every other way to (425) relieve some part of your despondency. But since bodily weakness and the illness assailing my head force me to stay home and keep me from such a beneficial service, I will not hesitate to bring, as much as I can, what remains to be done, both for your encouragement and for my own benefit. For perhaps there will be something further for you to bear the present things nobly. But even if I accomplish no such thing, at least leaving out nothing that depends upon me will make me better situated for the future. For the one who supplies everything that he thinks will bring release from the troubles that hold you fast, even if it comes to nothing, is from these arguments freed of blame and, laying aside the burden of accusation, is forced to bear only the burden of despondency.

If I happened to be one of those who are favored by God and capable of doing great things, I would not cease asking and praying for the person that I hold in honor. Since, however, the multitude of my sins keeps me from that confidence and strength, I will undertake to apply to you a consolation with words. For in the case of bodily ills, while doctors remove the pain and stop the sickness, those of the household slaves who are involved with the treatment are not kept from consoling, but they, more than anyone, lavish many words on their owners, should they happen to be loyal to them. For I pray that it may happen that I should say something capable of destroying this immeasurable suffering. But should I find nothing of this kind to say, he who through the blessed Paul urges us to "weep with those who weep and to join in with those who are humble"[1] will accept my readiness.

Therefore, there seems to be one cause for your despondency: the madness of this evil demon. One may find many griefs continually brought forth from this root. I am not now saying this of my own accord, but I often heard this for myself from your mourning when you were with me. First, that when you lived a more worldly life before, you suffered no such thing, but when you crucified yourself to the world, then you received the feeling of the sickness, which was enough to disturb you and throw you into perplexity. Second, that many who live in luxury, when they have suffered the same sicknesses as you, continued for only a short time, and then recovered from this weakness and returned to perfect health. They also entered into marriages, became fathers of many children, enjoyed the pleasures of the present life, and never again suffered any such thing. But *you* who spend so much time in fasts, vigils, and the rest of the training found no release from the terrors that held you fast. A third in addition to this: that the holy man who demonstrated so much power among other men was able to do nothing in the case of Your Love—neither he nor those who are with him and who are more powerful than he with respect to these things. But all of them departed embarrassed. And in addition to this, you also said that you suffered so excessively in various ways that the power of your soul was encompassed (426) with despondency, so much that you were often compelled almost to come upon the noose and upon the river and upon the precipice. And there is also a fifth reason for these things: seeing your peers, and those with you who lead the same life as you, pass their time in joy, while you lie in the roughest seas, and even now live in the most pitiable prison of all. For you said that it is not necessary to grieve those bound in irons as much as those who are af-

---

1. Rom 12.15–16.

flicted with this imprisonment. But you said to me that in addition to these there is another which disturbs you above all: that you fear and tremble over your father, lest he ever find out and do great and terrible things to the saints who received you in the beginning—that, trusting in power and in wealth, and being laid hold of by despondency, he might dare to do anything to them, and desist from nothing that occurs to him. And up to the present time, your mother has been able to conceal what happened and, having a strong attachment to you, often diverted him. But if the time approaches nearer for the pretense of your mother to be discovered, it will be unendurable for her and for the monks alike. But the height of evils is that you don't have courage for the future, as you do not see clearly whether there will then be a release and relief from this sickness, because you have often expected this and yet fall back into the same things again.

These things, then, are enough to disturb the soul and to fill it with much distress—but a soul that is weak, untrained, and sluggish. Should we, however, desire to see clearly for a little and to stir up pious thoughts, we might shake off these causes of despondency, as some light dust. Indeed, you shouldn't think that I stand outside of your toil and distress, that I easily promise these things to you now. For even if I appear to some to say unbelievable things, I will nevertheless say them. For you yourself will not disbelieve me, even if others do.

I didn't happen to be present (and I give thanks to our loving God) when that defiled demon first rushed upon your soul and threw you down to the ground among all while you were praying. But I learned everything with accuracy, as if I were present. For my friend and yours, Theophilus the Ephesian, came and related everything to me clearly: the writhing of the hands, the rolling of the eyes, the froth from the mouth, that ill-omened and obscure voice, the shaking of the body, the prolonged unconsciousness,[2] and the dream that appeared that night. He said that some wild boar, stained with mud, was continuously rushing upon you, and wrestling you. Then the

---

2. ἀναισθησία: this "lack of feeling/sense perception" can refer either to unconsciousness or to an insensibility to pleasure or pain.

one who sleeps near you was roused by the vision and awoke to find that you were again moved by the demon!

CHAPTER 2

When Theophilus brought this report, he poured a fog that is just as much for me as this demon is for Your Love. And when after a long time I recovered myself, the rest of this world's terrors seemed like nothing to me (427), nor did pleasures seem pleasant. But since I long ago became acquainted with the great vanity of worldly things, I was then affected by this much more, and a very great longing entered me for Your Piety. For such is the nature of painful things: its habit is always to intensify friendships. This is clear from the fact that they are easily able to bring feuds to an end. For it isn't possible that someone who sees an enemy suffering is so wretched or foolish that he will be able to hold onto his hatred of him. But if we have mercy on enemies and make friends when we see someone enduring something involuntarily, consider what I was likely to suffer when I saw him who is most beloved of all to me—whom I consider the same as my own person—suffering fatal injuries on account of despondency. Don't think that I stand outside your affliction, and don't, for this reason, view my consolation with suspicion. For if, by the grace of God, I have been delivered from being torn to shreds and from being thrown down by the evil demon, I bear the same share of the despondency and pain because of these things as you do; and let none of those who see me refuse to believe that I love as I ought to love.

Come, then, let's shake off the dust. For the nature of this despondency will thus be bearable and light, if only we don't wish simply to hand ourselves over to be dragged to the cliff's edge by the emotion.[3] Instead, let's hasten both to regain our senses and to reason as we ought.[4] For many of those things that seem to be great terrors appear unbearable before they

---

3. πάθος.
4. On hastening—or, really, zeal—as central to Chrysostom's moral/ascetic project, see Leyerle, *Narrative Shape of Emotion*, 150–82.

are scrutinized well. But if someone should examine these things with reasoning,[5] he will find that they are much less significant than suspected. And I hope that this will happen now. But rouse yourself, and do not make our enemy stronger by following the vain and irrational opinions of the multitude.

Now, if my discussion were to a nonbeliever, or someone who thinks all things happen by chance, or someone who attributes the providence of the world to evil demons,[6] it would require much work for me, so that, after I first expelled the deceptive opinion and persuaded him to recognize the true providence of all, only then would I turn the discussion to encouragement. But because, by the grace of God, you have known the holy writings from infancy and, as you received the true and saving teachings from your ancestors,[7] believe accurately that God cares for all, and even more for those who believe in him—because of this, let's omit this part, and make the beginning elsewhere.

When God made the angels—or, rather, let's bring the discussion earlier. Before the angels and the other heavenly powers came to be, God existed, having taken the source of his being from nowhere else. But always being self-sufficient (for such is the Divinity), he created angels, archangels, and the other incorporeal beings. And he created for no other reason than for goodness alone. For he neither had need of their ministration, nor would he have become the creator of these things, unless he was exceedingly good. And after the creation of these things, he made the human being—and the whole world—for the very same reason.

And he filled it with countless good things and established that small and simple one[8] for such great works, showing the human being to be the same upon the earth as God is in the heavens. For the verse (428), "Let us make the human being

---

5. Not with "reason" (λόγος) but with "reasoning" (λογισμός). This seems to mean something different for Chrysostom: it is a precise inquiry into causes. See Edwards, *Providence and Narrative*, 48, 139–42.

6. See Samantha L. Miller, *Chrysostom's Devil: Demons, the Will, and Virtue in Patristic Soteriology* (Downers Grove, IL: InterVarsity, 2020), esp. 11–45.

7. See 2 Tm 3.14–15.

8. I.e., the human being.

according to our image and likeness,"[9] means nothing other than that he assumed the rule of what is on the earth.[10] And when he had created him and established him in such great honor, God set apart the noblest paradise upon earth as if a kingdom for a king. In addition to this, wanting to show him from another point of view how much he surpassed the rest of the living things, God led everything to him and ordered him to give all of them names. And yet God gives him no help from among them. And he adds the reason: "There was not found," it says, "a help *like* him."[11] Having thereby taught him the distance between the natures,[12] and that he is more honored than all, and that nothing among so great a multitude is equal to him, God then creates the woman, honoring him yet again with this and making clear that she came to be through him, just as Paul also said, "For the man was not created through the woman, but the woman through the man."[13]

But God not only glorified him with these things, but also to him alone of all things did he give the gift of speech;[14] and God esteemed the human being worthy of knowledge of him and granted him to enjoy the benefit of discourse with him— as much as he was able to enjoy that benefit—and promised to furnish him with immortality, and filled him with much wisdom, and placed in him a spiritual grace, that he might even prophesy. And he gave him all these things when there had not yet been any accomplishment on his part.[15]

What, then, happened after so many and such great goods? The man believed the enemy to be more reliable than the one who had given all these things and disregarded the command of the one who made him; and he preferred the deceit of the one who hastened to lead him entirely astray and to expel

9. Gn 1.26.
10. On Chrysostom's distinctly Antiochene interpretation of this passage, see Carter, "Image of God in Man."
11. Gn 2.20.
12. I.e., between rational and irrational creatures.
13. 1 Cor 11.9.
14. Or "reason": λόγος.
15. On God's many gifts to human beings in creation, see Edwards, *Providence and Narrative*, 102–12.

him from all good things all at once. And, when the enemy showed him no benefit, either great or small, yet he preferred the one who offered him only words. Did God, then, utterly destroy him who showed such insolence from the beginning and, so to speak, from the first letter? For it would have been in accord with justice to destroy and throw out from his presence the one who experienced myriad good things and who, in exchange for these, immediately made the beginning of his life from disobedience and ingratitude. But God brought about nothing less than his earlier benefaction, showing that even if we sin ten thousand times and even if we turn from him, he does not cease to arrange what is for our salvation, so that we may turn again and be saved. And should we persist in evil, whatever God does is a consequence of this fact.

Therefore, it seems that being expelled from paradise, being kept from the tree of life, and being given over to death are done out of chastisement and punishment; but, as we have already seen, this is no worse than what came before. If what I am saying seems unbelievable, it is nevertheless true. For, while the events are contrary to each other, the ends of both are harmonious and in agreement. What I am saying is this: excluding them from paradise, settling them in another place, turning them away from the tree of life, punishing them, making them mortal, showing them that up to now they had been above exclusion—indeed, all these things, both the former and the latter—occurred for the same salvation and honor. (429) I don't need to say anything about what happened before[16]—for this is clear to all; but it is necessary to provide a discussion of what happened afterwards.

CHAPTER 3

How will we come to know that what followed was for his benefit? We should consider what he would have suffered, had these things not happened. What, then, would he have suffered? Since the devil had promised to show them after the

---

16. I.e., that what God did before the Fall—creation—was for the benefit of humanity.

transgression that they are equal to God, the man would have fallen into three of the utmost evils if he had remained in the same honor. He would have believed, first, that God was envious, a cheat, and a liar; second, that the one who truly cheated them—the father of falsehood and jealousy—was a benefactor and a friend; in addition to these, he would have continued immortal, committing sins for the rest of time. But God set him free from all these things when he threw him out of paradise. It is like this: when a doctor leaves a serious wound alone, he causes more putrefaction, but when he excises it, he prevents the damage of the wound from advancing further.

"So why," you might say, "didn't he stop here, but added 'sweat and toil'?"[17] Because this leaves nothing for useless relaxation—which is the nature of human beings. For if we don't stop sinning when "sweat and toil" are imposed, what wouldn't we have attempted if God had given us up to luxury and idleness? For it says, "Idleness taught every evil."[18] Both daily events and what came about in the time of our ancestors testify to this statement. "The people sat down," it says, "to eat and drink, and they got up to play."[19] And again: "He was made prosperous, fat, enlarged, and the beloved one kicked."[20] Blessed David speaks in unison with these when he says, "When he killed them, then they sought him out, and they turned back, and rose early to go to God."[21] And through Jeremiah God said to Jerusalem, "Be disciplined in every way, Jerusalem, so that my soul may not turn away from you."[22] And that being humbled and bowed down is not only for the salvation of those who are wretched, but also those who are good, the prophet says again, "It is good for me, Lord, that you have humbled me, so that I may learn your judgments."[23] And after this Jeremiah shouts out the very same things, even if not in

17. Gn 3.17.
18. Sir 33.27.
19. Ex 32.6.
20. Dt 32.15.
21. Ps 77.34.
22. Jer 6.8.
23. Ps 118.71.

the same words, "It is good for a man to take up a heavy yoke from his youth. He will sit alone and be silent."[24] And speaking about himself, he prays to God, saying, "May you be as a stranger, and spare me on the evil day."[25]

And although blessed Paul was so illustrious in grace and surpassed human nature, he nevertheless also prayed for the benefit of the same good. For this reason he said, "A thorn was given to me in the flesh, an angel of Satan, so that he might strike me, so that I might not be exalted. I called to the Lord for this three times, and he said to me, 'My grace is sufficient for you; for my power is completed in weakness.'"[26] And indeed it would also have been possible for the Gospel to triumph without persecutions, afflictions—"toil and sweat"— and yet Christ did not wish to spare preachers. For this reason he said to them, "In the world you will have affliction."[27] And he ordered those who desire to come to the kingdom to do this through the "straightened way,"[28] as they are not able to come there from anywhere else. Thus, the afflictions, the trials, and the painful things that befall us demonstrate to us the providential care of God no less than the good things.

And why should I speak of afflictions (430) here?[29] The threat of Gehenna demonstrates God's love for humanity no less than does the kingdom of heaven. For unless he threatened Gehenna, one shouldn't quickly obtain heavenly goods. For the promise of good things alone is not enough to persuade to virtue, unless the fear of terrors also pushes those who are more slothfully disposed towards it. For this very reason, he threw the first formed man out of paradise at the be-

---

24. Lam 3.27.
25. Jer 17.17.
26. 2 Cor 12.7–9. This seems to go against the sense of the verse, as Chrysostom here omits "that he might remove it from me" (ἵνα ἀποστῇ ἀπ' ἐμοῦ). Since Chrysostom includes this part of the verse elsewhere, it is unlikely that it is omitted from his biblical recension, and likely that he is, instead, quoting from it selectively to make his point.
27. Jn 16.33.
28. See Mt 7.14.
29. This paragraph is echoed nearly verbatim in *Stat.* 7.2 (PG 49: 94.7–18). See Introduction, p. 20.

ginning, since the honor given to him would have made him worse if it remained firm and steadfast after the rebellion against the command.

And why am I talking about Adam? For what wouldn't Cain have done if he had gone about in paradise and had enjoyed so much luxury? For in reality he was deprived of these things and saw his father's punishment up close, and yet he did not thereby come to his senses but fell into a greater evil, himself being the first to discover and to commit murder—and the most accursed murder of all. For he advanced to this new defilement not bit by bit, nor over a long period of time, but suddenly and unexpectedly he bounded straightaway to the summit when he lay in wait and destroyed the one with whom he shared his mother's labor, the one who did nothing wrong—unless honoring God is considered a fault.

But again, learn from me about God's love for humanity. For when Cain committed an outrage against him, God warned with words and consoled him who was suffering. But when Cain raged against his brother, then indeed did God proceed and execute the punishment. And the first[30] were deserving of the same punishment—or rather an even harsher one! For if in the case of human beings it seems to be a terrible thing and an insult when one of the household slaves keeps the better things for himself and brings the worse ones to the master, how much more in God's case! And Cain committed not only this sin but also another one just as great: being annoyed at his brother's honor. For if Cain changed his mind when he was sinning, he would have been approved for this very great change. But as it is, it was not mixed with repentance, but with both jealousy and envy—as the end even showed. For he was not only angry with God that after being insulted he didn't honor him; he also preferred the licentious one over the gentle one.

But while the sins demanded a very great punishment, God nevertheless furnished the one who had sinned with a much lighter punishment than was deserved, and he attempted to

30. I.e., sinning against God by not honoring him with a sacrifice and by envying his brother.

restrain Cain's enflamed soul. For that despondency was from anger. Therefore, he said to him, "Be silent."[31] And he said these things, seeing who would advance in evil, but wishing to cut out every excuse for those who are insolent.[32] For if he had punished Cain from the beginning, many people would have said many things such as this: "Wasn't it possible for God to encourage him with speech, and to counsel and reprove him beforehand, and then to pursue him if he persisted in these things? For that punishment was very cruel and harsh." For this reason, God endured the offenses against himself, at once bridling those who would say this while also showing that he trained Cain's father through his goodness; and he also leads those who came after these things towards and into repentance, through such kindness.

(431) And when, in accordance with his hardness and unrepentant heart, Cain had treasured up anger for himself, then he took vengeance. And if he had remained unpunished after the murder, he might have perpetrated a worse evil upon someone else. For we cannot say that he offended out of ignorance. How could he be ignorant of what the younger one understood? But if you want, let it be granted that he was ignorant beforehand. After hearing, "Be silent," and after obtaining pardon, from what ignorance did he set out to murder, and stain the earth, and overturn the laws of nature? Do you see now that the earlier things were not from ignorance, but from the utmost evil, wickedness, and defilement? What, then, was the punishment for these things? "You will groan and tremble upon the earth."[33] The punishment seems to be bitter—but not if we reckon the sin and really examine this punishment. For when he offered his sacrifice evilly, although he had insulted God, he was pained that he was not honored by the God who had been insulted; he spat upon the one who warned him; he was the first to commit murder—or rather a defilement much viler than any murder; he grieved his parents; he lied to God (for he said, "Am I my brother's

---

31. Gn 4.7.
32. I.e., those whom he goes on to speak of.
33. Gn 4.12.

keeper?").[34] And in exchange for all this he was only punished with fear and trembling!

And yet, I shouldn't say that God's kindness is apparent only in the lighter penalty for the sin, but also from its holding no meager benefit: the benefit was for all those who follow to be brought to their senses and to be improved through the rebuke given to him. It was for this reason that he didn't destroy him. For it wouldn't be the same to hear that someone named Cain, who destroyed his brother, died, as it is to see that the one who destroyed him paid the price. For, if that were the case, what was said would have been disbelieved because of the excess of the crime; but as it is, being clear and present, he made for himself many witnesses of the punishment over a long period of time and thus established that what happened is clear and credible for those at that time and those who followed.

"Then what benefit is this for Cain?" you might say. Above all, God gave careful thought to his salvation when he checked his rage beforehand (as much as possible) through words of encouragement. And if someone should scrutinize this punishment, he will also see that there is much benefit from it. For if God had killed him immediately, he wouldn't have given him any time for repentance and improvement. But at that time, when he lived in trembling and fear—unless he was exceedingly insensible and a beast instead of a man—he gained many things from this life.

Apart from these benefits, by this punishment he caused his future punishment to be smaller. For the grievous and punitive things that God applies to us in the present life prevent no small part of the tortures there. One may adduce witnesses of this from the holy Scriptures. When Christ was conversing with his disciples, he narrated what happened to Lazarus and said that Abraham was asked by the rich man to touch the tip of his finger a little to his burning tongue. And Abraham said to him, "Child, remember that you received good things in your life, and Lazarus, bad things. But now he is comforted

---

34. Gn 4.9.

here, and you are tormented."[35] And Paul—when I say Paul, I mean again the commands of Christ, for he moved that blessed soul—wrote a letter to the Corinthians at that time concerning one who had been fornicating (432) and ordered such a person to be "handed over to Satan for destruction of the flesh, so that the spirit might be saved in the day of our Lord Jesus Christ."[36] And speaking again to them about those who unworthily partook of the mysteries, he said, "For this reason, many among you are weak and sick and some have fallen asleep. For if we were judging ourselves, we would not be judged. But when we are judged by the Lord, we are trained, so that we will not be condemned with the world."[37]

Do you see God's ineffable love for humanity and the boundless riches of his goodness? Do you see how God did and accomplished everything so that even when we have sinned, we might be able to undergo a punishment that is gentler than we deserve, or even, at last, to be set free?

CHAPTER 4

But if someone should say, "Why didn't he do away with the deceiver from the beginning?" this is because he providentially cares for us so greatly. If that defiled one had overpowered by force, there would be some reason for asking. But if he has been deprived of that power and only persuades—and not being persuaded is up to us—why do you strip away the cause of good repute and cut off the reason for crowns? Additionally, if God knew that the defiled one was unconquerable and that he was about to overpower all, and yet allowed it, it wouldn't be worth puzzling over this. For even then it was up to us— we who were not forced but who willingly bowed to him—that the defiled one overcame and conquered. And yet this answer wouldn't be enough for those who want to be ignorant. But if there are already many who have prevailed over his power and again many who will have success, why do you rob of so great

---

35. Lk 16.25.
36. 1 Cor 5.5.
37. 1 Cor 11.30.

an honor those who will be approved and who will demonstrate a radiant victory? It is for this reason that he permitted it: so that those who were at first defeated by him might strike him down—which is for him greater than any punishment, and enough to lead him to the final condemnation.

"But not all will overcome him," you might say. And what is that to what we have been saying? It is much more just for those who are noble to receive opportunities in which to demonstrate their will,[38] and for those who are not noble to be punished from their own slothfulness, than for the former to be injured on account of the latter. For, in the one case, should the bad man be harmed, he isn't overpowered by his opponent but by his own sluggishness. The multitude of those who conquer him make this clear. But, in the other case, those who are zealous would be harmed by bad men, because on account of the bad men they have nowhere to make use of their bravery. It is almost as if a judge of athletic contests had two athletes: one who was ready to be engaged with the opponent, and to demonstrate much patient endurance, and to be wreathed in a crown, and another who preferred idleness and luxury to that exercise—and then he took the rival from the midst of the fight and sent both away from him, unsuccessful! (433) In this case, the zealous one is mistreated on account of the bad one, and the bad one is no longer bad on account of the noble one,[39] but on account of his own evil.

While it now seems that what was asked by them was about the devil, when this argument proceeds, it will consequently bring a charge against God's providence, and blame it for many things, and reproach the whole creation of God. For it will even accuse the way the mouth and the eyes were formed. It is because of this that they desire what is not necessary and many fall into adultery. Through the former they blaspheme, and others introduce destructive teachings. Is it therefore necessary for human beings to be without eyes and a tongue? Doubtless, we will also cut off our feet and sever our hands, since the latter are full of blood and the former run towards

---

38. Or the faculty of choice: προαίρεσις.
39. I.e., because he had been beaten by the noble one.

evil. Nor will the ears be able to flee the cruelty of this argument. For they also admit a vain sound and conduct defiling teachings into the soul—so let's get rid of these too! But if these, so also food and water, heaven and earth and sea, sun and light and moon, and the company of the stars, and every kind of animal. For how will these things be useful when he, for whose sake everything was made, is so pitifully cut up?

Do you see the silliness and absurdity to which this argument is forced to arrive? For the devil is evil to himself, not to us. If we wish, we may also bear much good fruit on account of him, which he neither wills nor desires. There is a greater miracle in this—even the excess of God's love for humanity. For the improvement of men harms the devil, and he truly grieves it! And when this improvement is introduced to us on his account, he will not be able to bear the insult.

How, then, is it introduced on account of him? When we have feared his cruelty, his incessant plots, and his successive machinations, we drive off much sleep, we are vigilant, and we have remembered the Lord through it all. That this is not my word, but that of blessed Paul, hear how he rouses the faithful who sleep with nearly the same words. Writing a letter to the Ephesians, he says this: "Our contest is not against flesh and blood, but against the authorities, against the powers, against the cosmic rulers of this age's darkness, against the spiritual powers of evil in the heavenly realms."[40] He said this not because he wanted to cast them down, but because he wanted to raise them up. And Peter said, "Be vigilant and awake; for your accuser the devil walks around, roaring like a lion, seeking to devour someone. For which reason, stand against him, firm in the faith."[41] He said this because he wanted them to work harder, and wanted to persuade them to have a greater kinship with God.

For the one who sees the enemy overtaking him runs all the more towards and comes close to the one who is able to come to his aid. So it also is that when little children see something fearful, they flee to their mother's breast, cling to her

40. Eph 6.12.
41. 1 Pt 5.8–9.

clothes, and cling fast to them—and even if many pull them off time and again, they don't give up. But when there is no disturbance, if the mother calls and tries to draw them over to her, they pay her no attention and even scorn her calling, and many of them turn aside to what is devised for their amusement and despise the table that she sets. (434) Therefore, since many mothers are unable to summon their children, they cleverly devise their return and convince them to run back to them again by fabricating bogeymen and bugbears.

This doesn't only happen in the case of children, but also in our case. For when the evil one scares or disturbs us, then we are brought to our senses, then we come to know ourselves, then we run to God with great haste. But if he was annihilated and done away with from the beginning, perhaps the many would not have believed what had come to pass—that is, that the evil one deceived the man and cast him out from those many good things. Instead, they would say that God did this from envy and jealousy. When there are those who dare to say this even now after so great a demonstration of his deception, if they never gained experience of his crime, what wouldn't they say? What wouldn't they utter?

And if it is altogether necessary to attend precisely to what happened, the devil does not push us to anything. Rather, while he does bring about many evil things, we also bring about many to ourselves by slothfulness and neglect alone. For, to return again to the beginning: when did the devil approach Cain and advise him to commit murder? Whereas the devil had appeared to his mother and conversed and furnished the deception, this is no longer the case for Cain—except if someone were to say that the devil suggested the evil thoughts. But even this would be from the one who had welcomed and been persuaded, and who made the way accessible to him in the first place! And yet God did not leave him alone, but continued to train and warn him, on account of which he seemed to punish him.

Why should I speak about the punishment of Cain—one man—when the flood, the destruction of so many men, is also able to display God's providential care to us? First, God did not simply introduce those terrors unexpectedly, but he even announced it beforehand—and not a short time before, but one hundred and twenty years earlier. Then, so that they might not fall into forgetfulness and slothfulness by the length of prediction, he prepared the ark to be constructed before their very eyes, which proclaimed God's threat more clearly than any voice. For Cain had already fallen out of human consciousness. But the ark, being laid before their eyes, continually awoke the memory of what was threatened. They, however, did not thus come to their senses, but instead continued to provoke and drag each other to evil things. God wanted neither to threaten nor to bring about the flood—nor even Gehenna itself—but it is we who are responsible for all these things.

A very wise person who comprehended this said, "God did not make death, nor does he enjoy the destruction of the living."[42] And God himself speaks through the prophet in this way: "For I would not desire the death of the sinner as much as that he turn and live."[43] But when we do not turn back, we bring destruction and death upon ourselves, while God, who does not want to destroy us, shows the way to flee from the devil.

(435) Is this all we have to say for the flood, then, and will we find that no benefit comes from it? But this would be to say nothing of the great advantage there was both for the very ones who died and for those who came after them. The former were prevented from advancing further in evil. But those who came after them gained more than they, when the leaven—that is to say, the very cause of evils—disappeared from their midst along with those who dared to do them. For if human beings could easily discover evil things without an example, what wouldn't they do when there are many around to encourage them to wicked deeds? So that this might not happen—that those who came after them might not have so many teachers of badness—he destroyed them all utterly.

---

42. Wis 1.13.
43. Ezek 18.23; 33.11.

CHAPTER 5

But what wise rationale—or rather foolish one—is there for wanting to do nothing good, but asking and saying everything to lay the blame for one's own sins upon God? "Unless God had allowed it," you might say, "the devil would neither have approached nor deceived to begin with." But Adam neither would have learned how much good he had, nor would he have ever come down from that madness. For he who esteems himself so highly that he even expects to become a god—what wouldn't this man have dared to do, without having come to his senses? Let's suppose that the devil had not advised him of anything, and that he hadn't spoken with Eve about the tree at all. If this hadn't happened, would they have continued without falling? We shouldn't say this. Even if the devil hadn't been there, he who was so easily persuaded by the woman would himself have fallen quickly into sin of his own accord. And this would have made his punishment even greater. And besides this, not everything in this case is from the devil's deceit, but the woman also fell when she was seized by her own desire. Scripture makes this clear when it says, "And the woman saw that the tree was good for food, and that it was pleasing for the eyes to behold, and that it was beautiful to contemplate. And taking its fruit, she ate."[44] I am saying this now not to free the devil from blame for his treachery, but because I want to show that unless they fell *willingly*, no one would have overthrown them. For the one who so easily welcomed deception from another was already disposed slothfully and frivolously before the deception. The devil wouldn't have been so strong if he had been speaking to a self-controlled and vigilant soul.

But there are some who, since they dispute this part, pass by the devil and go after the command. They ignore the one who sinned, while they bring a charge against God, saying, "Why did he give a command, when he knew that they would sin?" But these are the words of the devil and the inventions of impious thoughts. That the giving of the command is of

---

44. Gn 3.6.

greater providential care than not giving it would have been is clear from this: let it be that Adam has a slothful will[45]—as the end shows—and let him receive no command but continue to live in luxury. Would the weakness and slothfulness that comes from this relaxation yield something better or something worse? It is entirely clear that since he would be careless, he would have fallen into the utmost evil. For he who had no confidence in immortality, but saw that this hope was yet uncertain, was raised up to so much arrogance and folly that he even hoped to become a god, even though he saw no indication that the one who had promised these things was to be trusted. If he had been sure about immortality, how wouldn't he have come to madness?[46] (436) What sin wouldn't he have committed? Would he have ever obeyed God? But when you accuse God, you are like someone who blames the one who renounces fornication because those who will hear it would commit adultery! How are these words not of the utmost insanity? Even if the devil hadn't approached the one who received the command and hadn't advised him to abandon God, even this would easily have persuaded him: if he who disdained the one who gave the command after it had been given had heard altogether nothing from him, he would have quickly become ignorant of the fact that he is under a master. Therefore, God prevented this by what he had commanded and taught him that he has a lord and that he must obey him in everything.

"And what else came from this command?" you may say. Very many things! And even if nothing came about, this is not on account of God the teacher, but on account of the one who was not receptive to this very excellent education. But the gift of the command has not now, after the transgression, thus become useless. For hiding, confessing the sin, hastening to transfer the blame for what happened—the man to the woman, and the woman to the serpent—is from those who fear and tremble and recognize God's authority. No one is igno-

---

45. That is, the faculty of choice: προαίρεσις.

46. I.e. because there would be no consequences for his disobedience to God.

rant of how great a gain it was to be changed from that satanic expectation[47] to such great fear: for he who dreamed of being equal to God was so humbled and subdued that he trembled for fear of punishment and retribution, and confessed his sin. It is no small thing that he was not insensible to his sin, but that he quickly recognized and comprehended the offense. Rather, this is a path and a beginning that leads to correction and change for the better.

Therefore, while it is possible neither to learn nor to relate all the goodness of the Lord towards us, yet we do know its main point, so to speak. For after so great a disobedience, after such great sins, when the tyranny of sin held fast the whole world, when, finally, it was necessary to pay the greatest price and to be ruined completely, and for the race of men to become nameless, then he made a display of his kindness around us, slaughtering what is his own for enemies, for those who have been estranged, and for those who hate him and who turn their backs on the Only Begotten. By this he brought about for us reconciliation to him, having promised to give the kingdom of heaven, eternal life, and myriad good things, which "no eye has seen, nor ear heard, nor have entered into the human heart."[48] What could be equal to this providential care, love for humanity, and goodness?

Because of this, God himself says, "As far as heaven is from the earth, so far is my way from your ways, and my thoughts from your thought."[49] And mildest David, speaking about God's love for humanity, says, "As high as heaven is from the earth, so the Lord has increased his mercy for those who fear him; as far as the East is from the West, he has removed our transgressions from us. Just as the father has pity on his sons, so the Lord has had pity on those who fear him."[50] It is not that he is *only* this great, but that we do not know another (437) better example of the height of his affection—since Isaiah taught that it is even more than this. For he takes the

---

47. I.e., to "become like God, knowing good and evil" (Gn 3.5).
48. 1 Cor 2.9.
49. Is 55.9.
50. Ps 102.11–13.

mother as his model, who is more sympathetic to children than the father, and says this: "'Will a woman forget her children or not have mercy on the offspring of her womb? But even if a woman were to forget these things, yet I will not forget you,' says the Lord"[51]—which shows that God's mercy is above even natural affection. And while the prophets said these things, Christ himself, when he was conversing with the Jews, said, "If you who are evil know to give good gifts to your children, how much more will your heavenly Father give good things to those who ask him?"[52] He indicated by this nothing other than the fact that as much space as there is between good things and evil things, so much is the difference between God's providential care and that of fathers.[53]

But, again, don't stop here, but in your mind advance yet further! For what is said is only as much as you are able to hear.[54] For it is clear that just as his wisdom and goodness are infinite, so also is his love for humanity. And if we don't observe his love for humanity in each event, this is itself a sign of its infinitude. For day by day many great things are ordered for our salvation, which is clear by this alone: because he benefits our race by his goodness, and neither needs glory from us nor has use of any other reward, he allows very many things to escape our notice. But if he should ever reveal them, he does this for our sake, so that, being better disposed with thanksgiving, we might attract his aid. Therefore, let us give thanks to him not only for what we know, but also for what we do not know.[55] For he is well-versed in acting not only when we are willing, but also when we are unwilling. Thus, Paul, who also knows this, advised us to give thanks in everything and at all times.[56] And that he providentially cares not only for what

51. Is 49.15.
52. Mt 7.11.
53. For a close parallel to this section, see *Scand.* 6.7.7.
54. Here, as so often, Chrysostom highlights the limits—the weakness—of the human intellect, and its inability to comprehend the things of God. See Edwards, "Divine Incomprehensibility."
55. This prayer is also preserved in the eucharistic anaphora of the Divine Liturgy of St. John Chrysostom.
56. See 1 Thes 5.16–18.

is common to all, but also what is individual to each, can be heard again when he says, "It is not the will of my heavenly Father that one of these little ones should be destroyed"[57]—speaking about those who believe in him. For he wishes for all those who do not believe in him to be saved and to repent and believe, just as Paul also said, "He wants all people to be saved and to come to a recognition of the truth."[58] And Jesus himself also said to the Jews, "I did not come to call the righteous, but to call sinners to repentance."[59] And again through the prophet, "I desire mercy, and not sacrifice."[60] And when they enjoy the benefit of such great care and yet do not desire to become better and to acknowledge the truth, he does not thus abandon them. But when they willingly withdraw themselves from the life of heaven, he nevertheless supplies them with everything for the present life, making the sun rise upon the evil and the good, making it rain upon the righteous and the unrighteous,[61] and making available everything else for the existence of the present life. And if he exercises such great providence for enemies, would he ever overlook those who believe in him and serve him according to their ability? Not at all—not at all!—but he holds them with the greatest zeal of all. For he says, "Even all the hairs of our head are counted."[62]

CHAPTER 6

(438) And so, whenever you consider that you have cast from your hands your father, household, friends, relatives, unspeakable wealth, and much glory for the sake of Christ, and also that you now endure such great affliction, do not cast yourself down. From these reasonings your perplexity is born, and from the same reasonings will also be our release from perplexity. How? "It is impossible for God to lie,"[63] and

57. Mt 18.14.
58. 1 Tm 2.4.
59. Lk 5.32.
60. Hos 6.6; Mt 9.13.
61. Mt 5.45.
62. Lk 12.7.
63. Heb 6.18.

he promised eternal life to those who forsake these things.⁶⁴ And you forsook and spat upon all of them. What is it, then, that keeps you from having confidence in the promise? Is it the trial that now clings to you? But what is that to the promise? For he didn't promise us eternal life *here*. And even if he was about to fulfill the substance of the promise there, you shouldn't be so distressed. For the pious and faithful man should be disposed to God's promises so steadfastly that even if events appear to be opposed to the promises, he is neither disturbed by these nor despairs of the outcome.

Look now: faithful Abraham received a certain promise, but what was he forced to do? The promise was to fill all the world from Isaac, and yet the command was to sacrifice the very same Isaac from whom all the earth was to be filled. What then? Did this disturb the righteous man? Not at all. Rather, even when there was such great inconsistency and contradiction between the promise and the command, he was neither confused, nor did he lose his head, nor did he say something like this: "God promised other things and now must do those other things for me! He promised me that there would be a great multitude of descendants from this child, and now he commands me to slaughter him? How will this be, if the root is cut off? He deceived and tricked me!" He said none of these things, nor did he even consider them—and very reasonably indeed. For whenever God makes a promise, even if it seems that he destroys the promise ten thousand times, it is necessary neither to be disturbed with respect to the end, nor to question it. For this itself is certainly the work of God's power—to discover a way where there is no way—just as that blessed man reckoned at that time. For this reason, Paul was amazed by his faith, and said, "By faith, when Abraham was put to the test, he offered up Isaac,"⁶⁵ and he who had received the promises offered his only begotten. Paul indicates and hints at the same things that I have just said.

Not only Abraham, but his descendant Joseph, after a long

---

64. See Mt 19.29.
65. Heb 11.17.

time, also saw the promise endangered by many events and endured without wavering. For he alone saw what was promised. If he had fallen into human reasonings, he also would have despaired of the fulfillment. For the vision shown to him foretold his brothers and parents bowing down. But what happened was not like this, but very far from it! First, those who were going to bow down to him threw him into a pit and sold him to barbarian men, and they sent him to a very distant foreign land. In this way, what happened seemed to be opposed to what was made known to him—such that those wretched men even laughed at him and said, "Behold, that dreamer comes; so, come on now, let's kill him and throw him into one of the pits, and we will say, 'A wicked beast consumed him.' And (439) we will see what his dreams will be!"[66] And after this, those who bought not a free man, but a slave, handed him over again to be a royal slave. And up to this point, he had not yet endured terrors! But he encountered the mistress's slander and was condemned, and he lived in the prison for many years. Even after others had escaped, he remained there for a very long time. And while these things were very capable of disturbing his soul, he remained immovable to all of them.

Our experiences are of the same sort—and even much more difficult than these. For what was promised to us is the kingdom of heaven, eternal life, incorruptibility, and countless good things. But much of what has happened to us and come about in the meantime has been very far from these—for there are death, destruction, vengeance, punishment, and continuous, diverse afflictions. For what reason, then, did God do this and allow what is opposed to the promises to come to pass? He did this to accomplish two very great things: the one, furnishing us with an indisputable proof of his power—that it is possible for the promises to lead from being despaired of to the fulfillment; and the other, training our whole soul to believe in him, even if events appear to be opposed to what was said. For such is the strength of hope: it does not put to shame

---

66. Gn 37.19–20.

the one who clings to it purely.[67] For if those who received the promises back then were disposed in this way, we who do not expect the fulfillment of good things in the present life but in other ages must do this all the more. For Paul said this earlier in the same letter: it is "affliction and difficulty."[68] What is it that disturbs you, then? Why do you hold God's promise in suspicion? For disdaining the whole world because of this and saying, again, that he has no care for it is nothing other than being unfaithful and suspicious, and believing that that promise is a deception. This is what it is to be truly harassed by a demon, which calls forth fire from Gehenna.

But some who are turned over to the affairs of this life live in indulgence. Christ foretold the very same thing: "Amen, amen, I say to you that you will cry out and you will lament. But the world will rejoice."[69] And in the time of the earlier generations, the Babylonians, who did not know God, were in wealth, power, and honor, but the Jews were in captivity, slavery, and the utmost evils. And Lazarus, who was worthy of heaven and of the kingdom there, had sores and lay exposed to the tongues of dogs and continually battled with starvation. But the rich man was in honor, pomp, indulgence, and luxury. And yet, he neither enjoyed any of these things in Gehenna, nor was Lazarus hindered in the discipline of the present life by starvation or wounds.[70] But just like a noble athlete who wrestles in thirst and stifling heat, he overcame and was crowned. For this reason a wise man also says, "Child, if you draw near to serve the Lord, prepare your soul for trial. Make straight your heart and endure, and do not hurry in the time of affliction."[71] And after a little, he says, "In fire gold is tested, and human beings are accepted in the furnace of humiliation."[72] And again he says elsewhere, "Child, neither neglect the instruction of the Lord, nor be released from his

---

67. See Rom 5.5.
68. Rom 2.9. "In the same letter," because he had just alluded to Romans.
69. Jn 16.20.
70. See Lk 16.19–31.
71. Sir 2.1.
72. Sir 2.5.

reproof."[73] For the one who throws the gold into the furnace knows both how long it should be burned and when to pull it out. (440) For this reason, he says, "Do not hurry in the time of affliction."[74] And Solomon, teaching the very same thing, said, "nor be released from his reproof."[75] For great is the affliction—great for bringing the man to excellence and for training him in the virtue of patience.

"But why should he be overthrown and knocked down by the excess of affliction?" you may say. "God is faithful; he will not let us be tried more than we are able, but with the trial, he will make a way out for us to be able to endure."[76] For if discipline is out of love, and abandonment is from hate, it doesn't come, at the same time, from both loving and hating him, nor from both disciplining and abandoning.

"Then, how do many fall?" you may say. By withdrawing themselves from God, not by being abandoned by him! "For behold, those who distance themselves from you will be destroyed."[77] They distance themselves when they do not bear God's discipline but are instead angry and annoyed. They are just like worthless children who, when their fathers send them to teachers, flee the toils and a few blows there and depart from the sight of their parents. They gain nothing and entangle themselves in worse evils, and are forced to go hungry, to wander, to be sick, to be dishonored, and to be enslaved in a strange place. So also, those who don't bear God's discipline with thanksgiving, but who bear it ill, in addition to bearing no fruit from it, surround themselves with the utmost disasters.

For this reason we have instructed you to be steadfast and to make straight your own heart. But you have suffered extremely difficult things. For trainers do not train everyone in one and the same way. Rather, whereas they furnish those who are weak with weaker opponents, they furnish opponents such

---

73. Prv 3.11.
74. Sir 2.5.
75. Prv 3.11.
76. 1 Cor 10.13.
77. Ps 72.27.

as these for those who are noble. For the one who receives an opponent who has less than his own ability—even if he engages with him throughout the whole day—remains unprepared.

"Then how is it," you may say, "that he did not make those who have undertaken the same way of life[78] compete in the same toils?" Because there is not one form of training from God, nor do all need the same, even if they are in the same way of life. It is also the case that many who suffer from the same illnesses are not in need of the same medicines, but these of one, and those of another. Therefore, manifold and various are the ways of torment: one is tested with a long sickness, another with heaviest poverty, another with violence and injustice, and still another with witnessing constant and successive deaths of children and relatives. One is tested with exile from everyone and is allowed no conversation, and another is tested with reproof for he-knows-not-what, and with bearing the burden of a bad reputation, and another otherwise. For it isn't possible now to enumerate everything exactly.

And while each of these seems to be light and nothing in comparison to your own circumstances, if you were placed into their trial, you would learn that the one with which you are now stricken is much more bearable than those. And if there are also some who are disciplined less than we are, do not be scandalized on this account. For an increase in struggles is an increase in rewards and a sure support for no longer falling, whether voluntarily or involuntarily. It also reduces pride and turns away slothfulness; (441) it makes one more prudent and causes one to be more pious. And if someone wished to enumerate absolutely everything, he would find that there are many benefits of trials[79] and that there is no one who receives much esteem from God without affliction, even if it doesn't appear this way to us.

---

78. Here Chrysostom imagines Stagirius asking him why his fellow monks do not experience the same trials.
79. See *Stat.* 1, where Chrysostom actually enumerates the benefits of affliction.

CHAPTER 7

For if blessed Paul endured many a thing—and no one is greater than he, nor even equal!—how is it possible not to beg them for this help? But if some who are in these afflictions haven't been brought to their senses, this is no longer from the application of discipline but from their negligence. But if no medicine had been applied, the physician would seem to have destroyed him from lack of concern. But as it is, it is not at all the physician who is to blame, but rather the patients and their lack of attention. But if some who have walked upright before the trials fell after their application, while others who have practiced every evil were tried by no affliction at all, while still others have lived from their earliest age to their final breath being distressed with many misfortunes, we should not be disturbed nor fall on account of any of these. For if we who can and ought to know the administration[80] of his providence believed these things, it would be necessary to be despondent and disturbed. But if he who has communion with such great ineffable things and who ascended to the third heaven[81] became dizzy before that abyss; and if after peering out at the depth of the wealth of the wisdom and knowledge of God, he was only astounded and immediately withdrew, why do we weary ourselves in vain and concern ourselves with unsearchable things and seek what is inscrutable?[82] We don't contradict the doctor who orders things that seem to us to be opposed to what is profitable—who commands us to put the cool limb in the wellspring,[83] and who works many other paradoxes such as these. Instead, because we have convinced ourselves beforehand that he does this according to

---

80. οἰκονομία.

81. 2 Cor 12.2.

82. These sentences allude to Rom 11.33–36. See Edwards, "Divine Incomprehensibility."

83. He appears to employ this example because it is exactly the opposite of what was at Chrysostom's time the "conventional wisdom" of the medical profession, inherited from a humoral model of medicine (with its four elements: cold, wet, hot, dry) in Galen and, as he relates in *On Hippocrates' On the Nature of Man*, Hippocrates himself.

his skill, we readily yield. And indeed *they* are often entirely mistaken! Should we then inquire about God, who is so far removed from us in everything, who is absolute wisdom, and who never makes mistakes? And whereas we will simply believe the one from whom we should have demanded explanations, from the only one in whom it was necessary to believe we will demand proofs and explanations of what has happened, and we will protest our ignorance. How do these things belong to the pious soul? No, I ask and entreat us not to come to such great insanity! But in everything by which we may be perplexed, let's choose this: "Your judgments are a great abyss."[84]

Even this very fact is from God's wisdom: that we do not know everything clearly. For if we only trusted God after understanding the causes of everything that occurs, there would be no great reward for us, nor would it be a demonstration of our faith. But when we know none of these things and nevertheless love to yield to all his statutes, and come to genuine obedience and to pure faith, we benefit our souls very greatly. For it is necessary to be persuaded of one thing only—that all things are profitably applied to us from God—and no longer to seek the way, nor to be vexed or despondent that you are ignorant. It is neither possible nor advantageous to (442) know these things: impossible because we are mortal, and disadvantageous because it quickly leads to madness.

We do many things that appear to be harmful to our children, but that are nevertheless beneficial. And they neither expect to learn the reason, nor do we come to do it only after we first persuade ourselves that what happens is profitable, but we train them for this only: to yield to whatever their fathers order and to seek nothing further. Then, will we be so disposed to our parents, who are of the same nature as we are, and not be indignant, and yet be displeased with God (when there is so much distance between God and human beings!) because we don't know everything? What could be equal to this impiety?

Blessed Paul was indignant and said to such people, "On the contrary, O Man, who are you that you object to God?

---

84. Ps 36.6.

Does what is formed say to the one who formed it, 'Why did you make me thus?'"[85] And while I gave the example of children, Paul gave the much better example of the potter and the clay that was formed by him. Just as the clay follows wherever the hands of the one who forms it lead, so it is also necessary that the human being follow whatever God orders and receive with thanksgiving whatever God brings about, neither disputing nor being busy about learning it.

For these things are difficult not only for us, but also for those holy and wonderful men who came before us. For Job said, "Why do the ungodly live, and become old with wealth?" etc.[86] And blessed David: "My footsteps have all but slipped, for I was jealous of the lawless, seeing peace for sinners. For there is no upward movement in their death nor firmness in their torment. They are not in human toils, and they will not be tormented with human beings."[87] And after this Jeremiah said, "You are righteous, Lord, but I will speak of judgments to you. Why is it that the way of the ungodly flourishes?"[88] So, these very men were also confused and asked, but not in the same way as the ungodly, neither accusing God for what happened nor condemning him of injustice. For the one said, "Your righteousness is as the mountains of God. Your judgments are a great abyss,"[89] while the other, who suffered such great things, "did not render foolishness to God."[90] And in the middle of the book, Job related the incomprehensibility of God's wisdom and administration,[91] when he spoke about creation, and said, "Behold, these are parts of his way, and at the droplet of a word, let us listen to him."[92] And Jeremiah, foreseeing the very same thing, so that no one should be suspicious, pronounced his own judgment on the question,

---

85. Rom 9.20.
86. Jb 21.7.
87. Ps 72.2–5.
88. Jer 12.1.
89. Ps 35.6.
90. Jb 1.22.
91. οἰκονομία.
92. Jb 26.14.

saying, "You are righteous, Lord."[93] That is, "I know that all things happen justly because of you, but I don't know the way in which it happens." What more could they learn, then? But they did not obtain an answer to these questions. Blessed David, making this clear, said, "I thought how to understand; for this is a burden before me."[94] But he did not obtain an answer, so that those who come after these things might learn not to ask. And they asked only one thing: why do the ungodly have (443) well-being and wealth? Yet they didn't even learn this. But there are some who now inquire much more than they did. For the questions we have just set forth are much greater than those. Therefore, let the sure explanation of these things be committed to the one who "knows everything before it happens."[95]

CHAPTER 8

But if, because of those who pry excessively into these things, we must contrive some answer and consolation for those who inquire because of events which have already happened and which are well known to us, I would say this: the fact that the righteous are in affliction while the evil are in luxury is not, in the end, worth asking, now that the kingdom has been revealed, and now that the future age's reward has been shown to us. Since what is deserved awaits each person there, why is it necessary to be disturbed by the good or bad events here? God trains those noble athletes who are devoted to him with these labors; but those who are weaker and slower, and those who are unable to bear heavier things, he first urges on with the exhortation to good works.

But if the opposite things frequently come to pass—that many of the righteous live in luxury and honor, while the evil live in dishonor and the utmost evils—my first argument up to this point—which says that the righteous are mistreated and the unrighteous live in luxury—is overthrown by

---

93. Jer 12.1.
94. Ps 72.16.
95. Susanna 35 (OG).

this statement! But if it is necessary to resolve this, I would say this: God is not accustomed to arrange[96] things for us in only one way but is resourceful and carves out many paths for our salvation. Because many do not permit themselves to receive the proclamation about the future and the resurrection, he therefore shows here in brief the image of the judgment, when he punishes the evil and benefits the good. Whereas this will happen completely at the judgment, now it happens here in part, so that those who lose heart at that long time might become more yielding because of what is done in the present. For, if no one at all were punished for evil, nor honored for good, many of those who doubt the proclamation of the resurrection would flee virtue as if it were the cause of evils and would seek evil as if productive of goods. And again, if all were to receive what is according to what they deserve here, they may well believe the proclamation of judgment to be excessive and false. Therefore, so that the one might not distrust, and so that the large and confused populace who disdain might not become worse, he also punishes here many of those who sin and rewards some of those who are virtuous. By not doing this to everyone he shows the proclamation of the judgment to be trustworthy, and by punishing some before the judgment he rouses those who lie in a deep sleep. From the punishment of those who are evil many are roused by fear of suffering the same things; and from the fact that not everyone receives what is deserved, they are compelled to reckon that this has been postponed for another time.

For of course God, being righteous, wouldn't overlook that so many evil people depart without having been punished, or that so many good people are chastised with myriad terrors, unless he had prepared for each of them some other eternal dispensation. Therefore, (444) he punishes and honors not all, but some, just as in the time of the Persians, just as in the time of Hezekiah. Indeed, just as many in Assyria were impious, and many, like Hezekiah, were virtuous; but God did not treat them all the same. As I said, the reason for this is that the time of the judgment had not yet come. That this expla-

---

96. οἰκονομέω.

nation is not my own, hear from him who will judge us at that time. For when they approached him—those who brought the report of the death of those buried by the tower and the insanity of Pilate, which he displayed against those who had died by mixing their blood with the sacrifices—what did he say? "Do you think that these Galileans were sinners, compared with all the Galileans, that they suffered such things? No, I say to you; but unless you repent, all of you will likewise perish. Or those eighteen upon whom the tower fell in Siloam, and it killed them—do you think that these were debtors, more than all those who inhabit Jerusalem? No, I say to you; but if you do not repent, all of you will perish just as they did."[97] This is the reason for the delay. For this reason he is accustomed not to punish all those who are worthy of these things immediately, so that those who are left may become better by the misfortunes of others. And let these things be explained to us thus.

But you are probably asking about the things that were previously set forth, which are much more impenetrable than these. Since, however, those things are as clear to us as they can be, I think that through those I began to lay a foundation for the solution of these other ones. Therefore, what is it that you are confused about? That many, from the earliest age until death, struggle with many misfortunes? But, about these and the earlier things, I should also say that he punishes them, first, for their own evil, and, next, so that others may also benefit from the evils that befall them. But even if this doesn't happen in every case, it is not yet the time of the judgment.

Therefore, you may say, "Why are some punished before coming of age, when the good are distinguished from those who are not, as if they have committed great injustices?" There is not just one reason for this, but there are many different reasons: because of the lack of self-control of those who have been born, the slothfulness of those who tend them, inhospitable climates, and many other such circumstances. In addition to these, God knows that many of them will be evil,

---

97. Lk 13.2–4.

and so he restrains them beforehand with these punishments as if with shackles. Or don't you see that many who beg and who are in the same affliction cause very many terrors, neither from affliction, nor from famine, but from their own evil alone? For I once heard some men saying that they stopped a free and respectable woman who was alone and violated her. From what sort of need, from what affliction, does this deed come? And what terror would they not commit, if they were not held restrained by such chains?

And who would easily bear the insanity and the rage of those who live in prison? And those who are harassed by demons (445) causing nothing less than these! I am not talking about what they do at the time when they are harassed by the demon, but about what happens after this, when the frenzy stops. For they are also greedy, they steal, they get drunk, and they do much more shameful things than these. Therefore, it is just as in the case of criminals: the judge mostly leaves the multitude to live in the prison, such that they often end their life there. But when he wants to warn some of the multitude, he takes one or another of them and, sitting upon a raised platform, with everyone standing around, orders him to be put to death. He has no need to execute all of those who are evil to instill fear in those who remain. So also, when God wants to bring us to our senses, it is unnecessary for him to punish all who are bad; instead, seizing some of them whom he knows to be irreparable, he demonstrates his power and wrath, and from this achieves many things. For he thus encourages those who are evil, if they want, to make a change from their evil; he makes the good more attentive; he demonstrates his own longsuffering; and he makes the proclamation of the resurrection clear to all, as I said before.

Therefore, you may say, "Why do these things happen to those who are nourished with misfortunes in their early youth, and who breathe their last before they have arrived at distinguishing good from evil?" Tell me, what terror do these suffer, since they don't yet have knowledge of what they suffer, nor have they learned what grieving and rejoicing are? And I furnish not only this explanation for it, but also that from such misfortunes their parents, brothers, and relatives are brought to their senses. This gain is not small—from which the one is not harmed at all and the other benefits very greatly. And it is likely that there is some other ineffable reason, which is clear only to our Creator.

CHAPTER 9

One discussion still remains: why did those who walked rightly before the trials fall down after the trials? But who knows who walk rightly, other than he alone who "formed our hearts, and who takes note of all our works"?[98] For often many who seem to be good are eviler than all the rest. This is already shown in the present life, but in only a few cases, when some accident or necessity arises. And when he who "tests the hearts and minds,"[99] "who is living and active and sharper than every doubled-edged sword, who pierces to the point of separating soul and body, joint and marrow, who is able to discern thoughts and ideas,"[100] sits and judges us, then—indeed, then!—you will see not merely a few among the many, but all such people revealed. The sheepskin will not be able to hide the wolf,[101] nor the whitewashed tombs[102] hide the defilement inside. No creature will be invisible before the judge at that time, when everything has been stripped and laid bare before his eyes. Paul, making this clear to the Corinthians, said, "Therefore, do not judge something ahead of time, until the Lord comes, who will illuminate what is hidden in the darkness and make manifest the desires of our hearts."[103]

But, leaving behind the hypocrites, let us come to the discussion of those who live rightly. Where is it clear that they live rightly, if other things have been accomplished by them, but the chief good, humility, has been neglected? For this reason God let them go, so that they might learn that they were accomplishing these things not by their own power (446), but

98. Ps 32.15.
99. Jer 11.20.
100. Heb 4.12.
101. See Mt 7.15.
102. See Mt 23.27.
103. 1 Cor 4.5.

by the grace of God. But if someone says that it is better to triumph and to be lifted up than it is to be humbled and to fall, he is greatly ignorant of the harmfulness of arrogance and the benefit of humility. Know well and truly that a human being with madness, when he triumphs—if indeed he altogether triumphs—will immediately fall into the uttermost destruction. And the one who has been allowed to slip, when he has come to his senses from the fall, will be raised and very swiftly recover himself, if he wishes. But he who seems to do well with arrogance, if he suffers no terror, will not receive a sense of his own lawlessness at that time; but the terror will both increase and go unseen, when he departs from here empty. Just as that Pharisee, who went up and seemed to be rich in all good things, went down having learned that he was poorer than a tax collector.[104] But there is also another thing that is very powerful for laying waste to the good things that are acquired with much toil and sweat: the wind of vainglory. It is just like a wind that, when it enters, blows away all the treasures of virtue.

Look, then: there is yet another reason that has appeared to us about those who walk rightly—as you said. For there are many around us who have seemed to endure many toils for virtue and who are enduring; but since they look to honor from human beings and don't do everything for God, they are allowed to fall into trial, so that, having been robbed of glory from the multitude (for whom they have lost everything), and having learned that its nature is no stronger than a wildflower, they attend to God alone for the rest of their lives and do everything for him.

In addition to this, there are many more reasons for these things, which are invisible to us, as I said, but which are well known to God, who made them. Therefore, let's not be grieved at what has come to pass, but let's give thanks. For this is what right-minded slaves do.[105]

104. Lk 18.9–14.
105. The "right-minded slave" is a common expression in Chrysostom's ethical project—particularly with respect to those who yield to God's providence. See *Hom. Gen.* 31.4 (PG 53: 287–288); *Hom. Gen.* 39.1 (PG 53: 361); *Hom. Gen.* 47.2 (PG 54: 429–430).

And you are amazed that it wasn't before, when you lived luxuriously and you were clothed with worldly illusion, that this pollution assailed you, but that it happens now, when you have thrown off all these things and have dedicated your whole self to God. You act as if you were amazed that no one ever troubles the audience, but that, out of all the people, the opponent only approaches the one who is registered for boxing, who is trained, and who descends into the contest—and that the opponent only beats him on the head and punches him in the face. But it is not really amazing, nor worthy of despondency, if he afflicts, distresses, and oppresses us who were chosen to box. These are the rules of boxing! But if he overthrows you, casts you down, and comes away with the prize, this is what is terrifying. But so long as it is not permitted to come to this, not only will he do us no harm, but he will even benefit us very greatly by the hard struggle, thereby making us more honorable. And it is also the case that in the army the one who has many wounds to show, and who has taken upon himself single-handed combat against the strongest of the enemies, is better than all. We are amazed by those athletes who engage with "the invincibles"[106] (for thus they call the more competitive of the opponents)! And the hunter who is the most accomplished is the one who welcomes the beasts that are hardest to catch. (447) Isn't this demon ruthless and undaunted? Therefore, I do not stop being amazed and astounded by you: that having been allotted such an opponent, you neither fell down, nor yielded yourself, but remained unwavering, cast down from no direction.

CHAPTER 10

Accept, with my right to speak freely, what I am saying: I do not say these things now to flatter you, but you truly have borne the greatest fruit from this affliction. Otherwise, I wouldn't be able to offer a demonstration of it. Know and recall your former way of life, which was, as I said, before this trial. Scruti-

---

106. I can find no other record of such a group of combatants or competitors in Greco-Roman antiquity.

nize that way of life well, then, and contrast it to the present time following the trial. Then you will see the gain that has come to you from this contest. For now a great intensity has come about—in fasting, in keeping vigil, in zeal for reading, and in perseverance in prayer—and a very great softening and humbling has been accomplished. But formerly you had no discussion of the Bible, and all your care and toil were wasted upon the plants of the garden. I heard many laughing at your madness then, and blaming the splendor of your family, and the reputation of your father, and that you were raised in great wealth. But even you yourself know clearly your slothfulness in keeping vigil. For when others often arose straightaway at midnight, you yourself remained behind in the grip of deep sleep and were annoyed at those who awoke. But now all those things have been brought to an end, and have been changed for the better, from the time when you took up this fight and battle.

But if you ask me why God didn't allow this demon to assail you when you lived in luxury and when you were excited by the events of the world, I would answer that even this was out of God's providential care. God knew that if the demon discovered at that time that you were easily conquered, it would have immediately destroyed you. Therefore, God didn't summon this challenge straightaway when you came to the life of the monks but allowed you to be trained and to wait for a long time. I mean, once you became really steadfast, then he dragged you to the toilsome amphitheater.

Still, you will mention those who live in the world and bring your household slave to bear. For I know that you hint at this when you say that many worldly men who have fallen into this sickness receive a very swift and perfect (448) recovery. But, my dearest friend, your household slave and as many as have obtained this with him weren't in their case entangled with the same opponent as you are now. For to him and to others like him, God let loose this beast only to make them afraid and to make them better by fear; but for you, he did this so that you might contend nobly, overcome brilliantly, and win the crown of endurance. It isn't victory when someone, while the audience is still gathered, drags away the wrestler and takes him from the opponent, but when he allows the wrestler always to be engaged. So, if you were to wrestle and be led by despondency to irrational ideas, you would achieve nothing.

That this holds in your case, I syllogize well from the following.[107] It is clear to everyone, even if you want to be modest, that your life is so much better than that of your slave. Accordingly, your esteem for God and your attention to him are greater than his. This being clear, it is likewise apparent that even if there were an admission of hatred,[108] it would not extend to the one whom he loved more, even if he did immediately snatch away the much inferior one from the demon. And not only for this reason would I trust this, but also from those things which you seem to have abandoned—these most of all—will I attempt to demonstrate that God cares for you exceedingly. For if you hadn't made great haste and sent yourself on long trips in order to meet with holy and perfect men to release these chains, perhaps one would be greatly perplexed, since the cause wouldn't be at all clear as to why he allowed this for so long a time. But since you did come to the places of martyrs[109] where many—even those who eat human beings—have been healed, and you dwelt for a long time together with those miraculous and noble people who never sin, and, having ignored nothing whatsoever that might bring you deliverance from these sufferings, you returned having the enemy still with you, you brought back a clear and apparent demonstration to those who are really foolish with respect to God's providence for you. For he would not have thwarted so great a grace, nor would he have endured his saints being put to shame, except that he looks overwhelmingly to your good repute and, even more, your benefit. Thus, while this seems to be a sign of God's abandonment, it is a sign of his great affection and zeal for you.

---

107. What follows is an absurd argument, not one that Chrysostom actually grants.

108. I.e., that God hates him.

109. On the importance of martyr shrines in John Chrysostom, as it relates to his late antique context, see the introduction to Wendy Mayer's translation of Chrysostom's martyr homilies: *The Cult of the Saints,* Popular Patristics Series, Volume 31 (Crestwood, NY: St Vladimir's Seminary Press, 2006).

BOOK II

*His Consolation to Stagirius
and that despondency is even more
difficult than a demon*

ET ME SAY this about God's providence for us: that it neither deserts nor hates, but it loves exceedingly and trains in this manner. But since you said elsewhere that you suffer so much that the demon often coaxes you to go into the sea, or to throw yourself down from a precipice, or to destroy the present life in some other such way, I want to speak briefly about these reasonings. This advice is not only regarding the demon but also regarding your despondency. (448) In fact, it is concerning the latter more than the former—and perhaps concerning only the latter. This is obvious from the fact that many of those who are not harassed by demons resolve to do the same sorts of things from grief alone. Therefore, expel this despondency and cast it out from your soul, and that demon will have no strength left, not only to persuade you to these things, but even to propose it to begin with. For just as now, when, at nightfall, burglars snuff out the light and can very easily steal things and cut the throats of their owners, (449) so also the demon spreads despondency (instead of night and shadow) and tries to steal all the reasonings that lead to safety, so that it takes a destitute and helpless soul and wounds it with many blows. But when someone, by hoping in God, disperses this shadow, escapes to the sun of righteousness,[1] and hastens to give its beams to his soul, he will transfer the confusion from his own reasonings back

---

1. Cf. Mal 4.2 (3.20 LXX).

upon the robber. For when someone reproves criminals such as these and shows them the light, they become dizzy and are thrown into confusion.

And you may say, "How can someone be freed from such misery, without first being freed from the demon who causes[2] it?" It is not the demon that causes the despondency; rather, despondency is what makes the demon strong and puts forward evil reasonings. Here the blessed Paul may testify for us. For he feared not a demon but its immoderation, and he sent a letter to the Corinthians finally to spare the offender for the sin he committed, "lest such a person be swallowed up by more excessive grief,"[3] he says.

But if you want, let's suppose for now in our discussion that the demon urges you on, while despondency is expelled from your soul. What, then, will be the harm? What, by itself, could the demon do to harm us, whether great or small? But when the demon isn't present, despondency may cause many terrible things. We find that many of those who tie nooses, or who are destroyed by the sword, or who are drowned in rivers, or who destroy themselves in some other way, are pushed to these violent deaths by despondency. And even if some among them are harassed by demons, their destruction must be reckoned to be not from the demon, but from the tyranny and violence of despondency.

And you may say, "How is it possible not to despond?" It is possible, if you desert popular opinion about the matter and "set your mind on the things above."[4] For now, since the matter seems to the multitude to be terrible, so it seems to you. But if, having been released from this vain and erroneous preconceived idea, you desire to examine it as it really is with accuracy, you will find that there is no occasion for despondency, as has often been indicated to us already. But because of your peers (for I believe that it is when you see the brothers' gladness and open discourse that you are troubled and fall down), I would say this: if they lived in self-control and propri-

2. Literally, "moves": κινέω.
3. 2 Cor 2.7.
4. Col 3.2.

TO STAGIRIUS II

ety and in the rest of the philosophical life, while you yourself spent all your time in brothels and dice and revelry, the alleged reason for your despondency would hold some validity. But if you still walk the same path as they, then why do you suffer? For if my discourse were to someone else who was easily conceited, I would maintain silence about the things that I am now about to say to you. But since I am very confident that even if someone were to praise you and be amazed at you very many times, you would not, because of this, avoid moderation but would continue to order yourself among the last,[5] I will keep myself from nothing and say everything.

I hear that Your Piety's progress has been so great that your competition is no longer with children, but with great and amazing men. They say that you lack none of those things, neither with respect to fasting—for how are you surviving on only water (450) and bread day after day?—nor with respect to vigils, but rather that you prolong many successive sleepless nights in the same way. And with respect to your conduct during the day, they say that you already eclipse many of them. I also hear those who come from there tell me that all your time is taken up with prayer and tears. And just as some train[6] in silence or lock themselves alone in a hut and say nothing to anyone, so they say that you have done, going on for such a length of time. But they also shudder when they relate to me the affliction of your heart, the thirst, and the pain; and your affairs astound many from there who report, "He doesn't look anyone there in the face, nor does he cease from continually afflicting himself. Often we have feared that he will blind his eyes with lamentations or harm his brain with the severity with which he keeps vigil and with his steadfast and continuous zeal for reading."

CHAPTER 2

It is these things, then, that grieve and disturb you: that you have so greatly surpassed your peers and that, having a violent

5. Cf. Mk 9.35.
6. ἀσκέω.

and shameless opponent, you outdid those who ran with you by a great distance. Did I not fittingly say that despondency comes only from a preconceived idea, but when it is examined, it offers us many reasons for joy? For, tell me, of what benefit is not being harassed by demons, when one's life is neglected? And what kind of harm comes from being harassed by demons, when one attains to scrupulous and well-disciplined ways of living? Perhaps you blush in shame when it throws you down in the presence of others? But this happens to you for this very reason: that you entrust the event to popular opinion, and never to reasoning. For this falling down isn't what you say you suffer, but falling into sin—in which case it would be good to be ashamed and pained at this fall.

And we now sink in sadness over those who have no shame, while we believe that we suffer nothing terrible when we do things that are truly shameful and full of much derision and the utmost punishment. But when the soul day by day falls under sinful actions, no one grieves, while if perchance the body suffers something, it seems to be terrible and unbearable. Isn't this being harassed by demons: the soul being so disposed and erring in the judgment of events? For if you suffered this because you were drunk, it would be necessary to sink in sadness and despond, for the fault was by choice.[7] But if the event is due to someone else's force, neither the one who is abused nor the one who endures violence ought to be ashamed, but the one who acts. For if it happens that when there is a fight in the marketplace, someone shoves and throws another person down, we all blame the one who threw him down, not the one who fell. Blushing is good, but only when we do something that brings punishment upon us from him who will judge us in the future. So long as we aren't aware of such things in ourselves, should we therefore be ashamed? No! For if someone arrested you and openly beat you, having nothing to accuse you of—or, again, if he threw you down to the ground—and, bearing all this mildly, you were to recover, it wouldn't be something shameful, but something philosophical and to your greatest praise. (451) Accordingly, when men abuse you,

---

7. προαίρεσις.

that you bear the ill treatment is a commendation; but when the one who is more wicked than anyone does the very same thing, will he who nobly bears his madness shrink back as if he were committing a blameworthy deed? What could be more irrational than this contradiction? For if, after getting up from that fall, you proceeded to do or to say something wicked, I myself wouldn't hinder you from being stricken and in pain on this account. But if you bear all things with thanksgiving, and you immediately turn yourself to prayer, what did you do that was shameful?

"But perhaps reproach from others is painful." Who could be more shameful than those who are unable to see properly what they must be ashamed of? Those who are truly mad and harassed by demons are those who haven't learned to see things as they are in nature, but who censure what is worthy of praise and transpose the most shameful things into the class of what is praised. Those who are sick with phrenitis say many nasty things to those present, but those who hear them don't think they are being insulted. Therefore, when you hear those senseless things, you shouldn't consider them to be a disgrace or an insult, so that you may not make yourself truly shameful and provoke God. For when you think what is applied by God for instruction and benefit is a disgrace, see where the evil ends!

CHAPTER 3

If you want to know who is truly worthy of shame and reproach, I will try with my discussion to show you a few out of the many. Look at those who are excited by the beauty of women, those who are crazy about money, those who lust for power and glory, and those who choose to do and to suffer everything for these things; those who are consumed by envy, those who plot against people who have done nothing wrong, those who simply suffer from melancholy,[8] those who

---

8. Here he appears to distinguish between *athumia* that he has been discussing and *melancholia*. Although the difference is not clear, *melancholia* was well established as a medical condition in Galen and the Hippocratic corpus, and at

are always frenzied about life's vanities. These and such things are works of madness and worthy of punishment; these are shameful, disgraceful, and ridiculous. But if someone is troubled by a demon and even so displays much wisdom[9] in his life, not only would it be right not to be ashamed, but also for all to marvel at and crown him, since he runs so difficult a race in such great chains and ascends the steep and rocky way of virtue.

But I don't know how something else has almost escaped my notice, which you have more of a claim to than the brothers—namely, that if there has been some offense committed by you, these sins are easily stripped away by this affliction. That this happens to us has become clear from what I already said, when I spoke about Lazarus and about the fornicator among the Corinthians.

But you may say, "I have been afraid because of my father. Even if I can meekly bear my own misfortunes and madness, how will I bear them easily if he learns something of them?" He hasn't sensed it for now. But it is truly small-minded to reap the fruit of despondency now or to beat your breast, because of what may happen later or what will never happen. For where is it evident to us that he will find out? Or, rather, let it be clear, and let it be allowed—if you wish—that he will learn of it and he will bring about great terrors. I would praise you for suffering (452) on account of his evils, but I don't think it is right to do this along with your own harm. For, it is necessary for those who mind the things above[10] and not the things upon the earth to rule over not only anger, desire, and the other passions, but also over despondency.[11] For despondency will bring about even greater terrors than those passions, and you must stand up to it nobly lest it destroy you completely. For if you yourself were to be the cause of painful things befalling your father, you would do well to

---

least in the former was often associated with Stagirius's other condition: epilepsy. See Leyerle, *Narrative Shape of Emotion*, 90–91.

9. φιλοσοφία.

10. See Col 2.3.

11. Here, as in *Stag.* 3.14, he brings together θυμός, ἐπιθυμία, and ἀθυμία.

fear and tremble, since you would be responsible for so much destruction. But if he wants to pierce himself with the utmost evils, there is no reason for these things to affect you, except as much as you ought to sympathize with your father. But apart from these things, we don't know how he will bear this news. For many things have often turned out contrary to expectation. And while the one reaction would be unexpected and unusual, the other is both likely and very possible.[12] From where is this clear? He holds his illegitimate children in high esteem, and his affection for them is enough to obscure his despondency.

Do not distress yourself with these concerns for no reason. But if it really is necessary for you to suffer because of your father, do so for his irrational expenditures, feasts, vanity, tyranny, and ongoing adultery. Or do you think defiling himself with another girl—when your mother is at home—and begetting children from lawless marriages is an insignificant evil? These things are worthy of tears, these, of crying—evils which are manifest, and which have passed beyond the limit. And the things that will befall you might or might not be terrible, but it is highly irrational to endure the accepted torment now for things that are so uncertain.

And should we grant that these things will be met with great severity, it will nevertheless have the quickest of ends and will be quenched before it has even been properly kindled. For a man who devotes himself to such luxury, who manages many affairs, who feeds hangers-on and flatterers, and who is so inflamed with desire for that girl from whom he has your half-brothers—even if he learns of your affairs, it will strike him as insignificant and of little import. I make this guess not only from what I have said, but also from what has already happened. For you know—you know clearly—that, although he loves you exceedingly and considers you his crowning achievement, since you departed to the life of the monks, he quenched all that love and thought it a shameful

---

12. Chrysostom seems to be turning Stagirius's expectations on their head: that his father is likely to react happily to the news (as Chrysostom suggests below), rather than angrily.

thing, unworthy of the eminence of the firstborn, and he said that you disgraced his reputation. Without the force of nature holding him back, he would probably also renounce you. So, if what I have said isn't exceedingly stupid, I think that he would even be pleased with what has happened, as if you are paying the price for the life of this endurance which he often advised and counseled you to abandon, and you did not, as far as words, accept the advice.

CHAPTER 4

This is what I would say about your father and the fear you have had on his account—and it is enough, I think, to relieve every fear that has come over you because of this. Since you were saying that the chief evil is that you aren't confident about the future—that you do not know whether there will be some relief from these things or whether the one who has given you this contest will want you to contend until death (453)—I myself have nothing accurate to say about this, nor to reveal about the future. I do, however, know this clearly and I think it worth persuading you thus: that whatever comes of these things, it will be profitable for us. And should you be so disposed, the chief evil (as you say) will be driven away quickly. In addition to this, it is necessary also to reckon that the time for prizes and crowns is the age to come, but the present age is for sweat and struggle. Blessed Paul wanted to make this clear to us and said, "I run not as if I am uncertain. I contend not as if I am beating the air. Rather, I strike and enslave my body, lest, having proclaimed to others, I myself become worthless."[13] But when he drew near to death, he then let out that blessed utterance, "I have fought the good fight, I have finished the race, I have kept the faith; finally, the crown of righteousness is set aside for me,"[14] showing that it is necessary for all our life to be strenuous and laborious, if indeed we would come to enjoy the benefit of eternal rest and myriad good things.

13. 1 Cor 9.26.
14. 2 Tm 4.7.

But should someone slothful wish to enjoy the benefit of both the pleasures here and the rewards laid up for those who toil, he will cheat and deceive himself. It is just as in the case of athletes: the one who is interested in relaxing during the contest gains for himself shame and ill repute for all time, but the one who nobly bears every toil in the stadium enjoys from the audience crowns and glory and admiration, both in the contests themselves and once they are over. So also in our case: the one who makes the time for toils a time of rest, when he needs to enjoy that eternal rest, will then wail and gnash his teeth and suffer the utmost terrors. But the one who has willingly borne afflictions here will be illustrious and glorious both here and there—a glory both undying and true.

For if, in the case of worldly things, the one who upsets the good order of things will be excluded from every appointment and surround himself with very many misfortunes, in the case of spiritual things much more will the one who does not know the order of times suffer this. Christ said, "You will have affliction in the world."[15] And blessed Paul said, "All those who desire to live piously in Christ Jesus will be persecuted,"[16] speaking not only about persecutions from human beings, but also the plots of the demons. Job said, "Life upon the earth is a human being's trial."[17] Why, then, are you distressed when you are afflicted in the time of hardship? For then it would really be necessary to suffer, if we make this time of affliction, which Christ spoke about before, into a time of luxury and rest—if when we are appointed to contend and to toil, we have instead reclined; if we walked the broad way, when he ordered the narrow one. For in that case our being punished in that age would follow from necessity.

You may ask, "What would you say about those who walk here along the broad way and who will also rest there?" Who is this person? For I believe only in the word of Christ, when he says, "Narrow and crushed is the way (454) that leads to

---

15. Jn 16.33.
16. 2 Tm 3.12.
17. Jb 7.1.

life."[18] It is clear to all that it is not at all possible to walk the narrow way with ease. For whereas, in the case of external contests, no one is crowned with a wreath without sweating, even when they have opponents who share the same nature, how is it possible, when the evil powers rebel against us, to overcome their madness without affliction and difficulty?

CHAPTER 5

But for how long should we scrutinize these things from reasoned discussions,[19] since we are able to take refuge in those blessed and noble athletes who existed in earlier times? Scrutinize all those illustrious men from that time, and you will see all those who, from afflictions, held free discourse with God. Indeed, if you wish, let's come to the child of the first-formed man, the lamb of Christ, Abel, who committed no injustice but endured the most terrible deeds. For with trials we pay the penalty for sins, but that righteous man was chastised for nothing other than being righteous. And so long as he did nothing great, his brother approved of him. But when he became illustrious from the sacrifice, his brother disregarded his own nature and was blinded by envy. Therefore, how do you know that this same cause hasn't even now roused the devil, and the luster of your life hasn't incited him to this battle? But if you would laugh at my words, I would praise you for your humility—indeed, I wouldn't stop feeling this way. For if Abel offered fat and was therefore highly esteemed, how much more would one who offered nothing external to God, but only his whole self, have provoked the enemy against himself! And God allowed him to advance. For he didn't prevent the murder from occurring at that time but allowed the righteous man to fall into the hands of the bloodthirsty man, and he didn't snatch away the man who by himself rescinded the honor that was given to him. For God did not want to diminish Abel's crowns. For this reason, he allowed Cain to advance to the end.

18. Mt 7.14.
19. λογισμοί.

And you may say, "What sort of punishment is death? Oh, how I have been waiting for that punishment now!" You say this now, beloved, but at an earlier time the event seemed to be the most difficult of all and more pitiable than every penalty. For this reason, in the Law of Moses, those who committed the greatest injustices, which were too great to be pardoned, endured this punishment. And even now among the worldly lawgivers, all those who are convicted of the most shameful crimes are punished in the very same way. But, whatever the case, the righteous man suffered the same things as the lawless—or rather something much harsher, inasmuch as he received the blow from his brother's right hand.

And what about Noah? For this man was both righteous and perfect, and when all were corrupt, only he was pleasing to God, while all others were offensive to him.[20] Therefore, he endured very many afflictions—many and evil. For this man didn't die immediately, as Abel did—he didn't suffer what seems light to you—but he endured a long life, and for so many years he was continually situated in nothing better than bearing and being pressed down by the heaviest loads. I will now make Noah's affliction very clear to you, since I already spoke about that of Abel.

He lived in a prison for a whole year—a prison strange and fearful. I pass over the multitude of beasts and creeping things with whom he was yoked together for so long (455) while he was enclosed in such a small space. What do you think he suffered from the claps of thunder, from the sound of the rain? The abyss below gapes wide, and the one above bears down hard. And he sat inside with only his sons. Even if he had confidence in the end, he would nevertheless have died before his time from fear by the violence of events. For if we, who have homes anchored to the earth and who inhabit cities, see just a little more rain bearing down than we are used to nevertheless drop down and cower, what wouldn't that man have suffered while he was alone inside, thinking of that most awful abyss and various kinds of suffocation? One city or one house being flooded and covered with waves would

---

20. See Gn 6.9–12.

be enough to perplex a soul, but the whole world suffering this—I cannot say how it would have disposed him who was carried around in the midst of waves. He was thus held fast by so much fear for the entire year. When the flood ceased, his fear finally receded. But his despondency increased, and another storm, no less than the first, overtook the one who emerged from the ark, when he saw the great desolation, that violent death, and the bodies of those who were destroyed, planted in the mud and mire—all the men and donkeys together, and species more dishonorable than these, buried in one most pitiful grave. Even if those who suffered these things were exceedingly sinful, Noah was nevertheless a man, and he suffered for his compatriots.

When Ezekiel, who was righteous and who saw that the Israelites were the most wicked of all, saw them being slaughtered and falling, he also suffered this together with them and wept. Indeed, it was for this reason that God—since he recognized this beforehand—revealed all their impiety to Ezekiel and prepared his eyes to observe it, so that when he saw them suffering, he might bear the calamity nobly. And yet even when so great a consolation was prepared for him, he was so overcome that he fell down and cried out, saying, "Woe is me, O Lord! Are you wiping out the remnant of Israel?"[21] He suffered this not just once, but also again when he saw Jeconiah[22] being removed. So also Noah, even if he was privy to ten thousand of their evil deeds, was braver than neither Ezekiel nor Moses. For even if he had often suffered the same things as the prophet and had seen them sinning, when it was necessary that they be punished, he suffered—or rather was tormented—because they were punished. But at Noah's time, the calamity was even harder to bear. For only that man experienced such a death.

Now, on him who was subject to so many evils—solitude, suffering for his kinsmen, the vast amount of destruction, the way of death, the desolation of the earth—and when in every way despondency was growing and blooming exceedingly, his

---

21. Perhaps a paraphrase of Ezek 11.13.
22. Also known as Jehoiachin; see 2 Kgs 24.15 and 2 Chr 36.10.

child's[23] offense was immediately inflicted—an unbearable thing, full of much shame and misery. For, just as shame that comes from friends is heavier than that from enemies, so these same things are even more unbearable when they come from children. For when he sees the one whom he fathered, nourished, and trained, and for whom he endured much labor, toil, and solicitude, treating him in a way that is more offensive than all (456), he who suffers this won't be able to bear the great grief of his soul. For the offense in itself is unbearable from free men, but when it also comes from children, it would even lead the sufferer to astonishment. In this way it is the heaviest.[24]

And don't only consider that shameless deed, but also learn from this how this offender treated Noah during all the time before the flood. He who still had the fear of what had happened close at hand, when he was only just free from that prison and still looked at the misfortunes of the whole world, didn't thereby come to his senses, but instead offended against the one whom he should have least of all.[25] And he became better neither by the death of many, nor by the desolation, nor by God's anger, nor by any of the other things that happened at the time. Who was this man before the flood, when he had many to encourage him to evil?

For then—then indeed—did that righteous man endure a wave more difficult than those that happened after this during the flood, on account of both this one son and everyone else. For at the time of the flood it was only a multitude of waters that surrounded him, but before this he was subjected to the abyss of evil from every side, and the plots of evil men dashed against him more violently than any wave. For he alone was left behind with so great a multitude of lawless and polluted people. Even if he suffered nothing terrible, he nevertheless bore much ridicule and derision (if not before, at least when he spoke to them about the ark and the coming calamities). And let him who was sanctified from the womb

---

23. Ham. See Gn 9.20–23.
24. Referring to his comment earlier at the beginning of the paragraph.
25. I.e., his father.

testify to us how much power this has to disturb the soul—and who for this reason was about to abandon prophecy. For it says, "I said, 'I will not prophesy.'"[26] Apart from this, if there were only this—that he had no one likeminded nor of the same manner of life—how much displeasure, how much despondency would this have furnished him with?

And he suffered many terrible things, not only this but also by sharing in their pain. For the righteous are doubtless pained not only when they observe those who are evil dying but no longer sinning, but they are stung much more by their sinning than by their dying. One may learn this well from the prophets. For one cries out bitterly, "Woe is me, O my soul, that the pious person has perished from the earth, and the upright is not among human beings."[27] And another said to God, "Why did you designate me to oversee toils and troubles?"[28] And mourning exceedingly for those who were harmed, he lamented, saying, "You will make human beings as the fish of the sea who have no leader."[29] But if these things happened at that time, when there were laws, leaders, law courts, priests, prophets, and punishments, then consider with what excess everything was undertaken in the time of Noah, when none of these things bound them. And in the time of the prophets, the span of life wasn't long, but seventy or eighty years. But the life of this man stretched to six hundred years and more. Therefore, so that I may avoid saying everything: (457) how much was he forced to bear when he journeyed such a long way and took pains not to turn aside even a little for so long, when they were in the midst of many waves? And why do I speak of *many*, when *the entire way* was so thoroughly like this—when from one end of the earth to the other, everywhere was full of rocks, thorns, beasts, drought, plague, frost, and criminals? For it would be easier to journey on a beaten path at midnight anywhere than to walk the way of virtue in those times, so many were those who were pressur-

26. Mi 2.6.
27. Mi 7.2.
28. Hab 1.3.
29. Hab 1.14.

ing his footsteps to stray. For when it was possible for all people to do whatever they wanted, and he was the one and only person going against them, how would he be able to reach the finish, with everyone forcing him backwards and pushing back against him? How difficult it is to live virtuously with many around you is made clear by those who now undertake to live in solitude, when, by the grace of God, it is possible to see well-being sown everywhere and there is no little concord and affection for one another. But at that time there were no such people, and all people were disposed towards Noah more fiercely than beasts.

CHAPTER 6

What, then, could be more distressing than this life? What more wretched than this life? So, while I promised to show that Noah was no better off than those who are always bearing burdens and never breathing easily, the discourse did much more than this: not only did it show us that he was no better off, but it also showed us that it was much more burdensome for him than for them.

Therefore, Abraham seems to many to have spent all his time in joy, for which reason they are accustomed even to attribute to him cheerfulness and continual flourishing. But, come, let's scrutinize what happened to him. For, in my view, this man experienced much more than both Noah and Abel. But I would rather say nothing until the close scrutiny of the events casts our vote. No one would be able to know clearly his affairs in Persia—even if something grievous had happened up until the time when he was seventy years old. For blessed Moses did not write for us the history of that time but left aside this whole period of time and made the beginning of his narrative from what happened after this. But it is no longer unclear that, similar to the others, he likely suffered the same things as Noah, wishing only to be pious in the midst of such impious barbarians. Even those who are exceedingly ignorant might easily guess this.[30]

30. Chrysostom here seems to be aware of some of the apocryphal traditions

But let's pass over this for now and instead take the beginning of the discussion from his travels. Let's scrutinize this first: how far the land of the Chaldeans was from Palestine, how much equipment was needed for the journey, how he was situated with respect to his dealings with other men, and what the manner of his life was. For don't think that, just because that righteous man obeyed easily, the deed was easy, nor that because Moses narrated the event briefly and succinctly, the brevity of the words is in imitation of the deed. For to say and to relate these things is easy, but the deed is in fact exceedingly hard!

Therefore, whoever walked to us from there,[31] if indeed there are any, would be able to state precisely the length of the journey and how great a distance there is between these countries. (458) I have spoken with none of them, but instead with someone who arrived from a very distant country, and I asked him how much time is needed to make the journey there. And I heard that the number is thirty-five days. He said that he didn't see Babylon, but from those who had been to Babylon he heard that from where he was, there was again as long a journey.[32] And the distance at that time was just as great as it is now. But the construction of the roads is no longer arranged in the same way now as it was then. For in our time it is marked at intervals with continuous way stations, cities, and farms. And one may happen upon many travelers while walking, who are no less a cause for safety than a way station, city, and field. In addition to this, leaders of the cities marshal men from the country who are superior to others in bodily strength, and with javelin and sling, and who are as

---

surrounding the patriarch and then intentionally to omit them. On his knowledge of these traditions, see Demetrios E. Tonias, *Abraham in the Works of John Chrysostom* (Minneapolis: Fortress, 2014), 55–56, 84.

31. I.e., from Persia to Antioch.

32. I.e., it takes seventy days to get there. According to "ORBIS: The Stanford Geospatial Network Model of the Roman World" (https://orbis.stanford.edu), which can only calculate as far from Antioch as Dura, the fastest means of transport would take 22 days; with the least expensive means it would take 53 days from Dura to Antioch. Though Chrysostom does not mention where his traveler friend came from, his calculation is hardly an exaggeration.

capable of defending as archers with arrows or soldiers with spears; and they set superiors over them and spend their time on nothing else, but are entrusted solely with guarding the road. And besides this, they contrive again another more complete assurance against danger: they construct buildings at an interval of a thousand steps along the way and establish nightly watches at them, fortifying their vigilance and attention into the greatest defense against the approaches of criminals.

But at Abraham's time, there were none of these things: neither successive farms, nor cities, nor way stations, nor lodgings, nor easy-to-see fellow travelers, nor any of these other things. For I now pass by the ruggedness of the path and the inhospitable climates, which, even when the other things I mentioned aren't added, are enough to grieve those who make the journey. And those who use chariots and donkeys may testify that they don't dare to go upon the common path unless they first spread stones on it and fill up the gullies made by mountain streams, and thus level them out. But at that time it was more desolate than uninhabited places, more impassable than the mountains, and more perilous than pits and precipices.

I haven't mentioned the most difficult thing of all: how Abraham's dealings were disposed, which, more than the journey, furnished many more and greater difficulties to them, nation after nation—or rather city after city, since all were divided. For at that time it was not as it is now, with one empire stretched over the greater part of the world, with all serving one man, and being administered according to the same laws. But like a single body cut into many parts, so also the human race was torn asunder, and the righteous man was forced to exchange one enemy for another. And before fleeing the first, he was always running into others. Where there are many leaders, there is anarchy.

Therefore, what could be more difficult than this life? For he didn't fear and tremble for himself alone, but also for his father, his wife, and his nephew. And he had no small concern for his household slaves—even if they were in his own land, let alone when they were forced to be continually in foreign lands. And if he had known clearly where his wanderings would cease, his anxieties would not have been so unbearable. But as it is, he heard simply and without qualification, "a land"—not this or that land, but one "which I will show you."[33] And he went about (459) everywhere in his mind and took into his soul a great disturbance. And in his thinking, he was not able to settle anywhere but had to be suspicious about many things and was forced to be anxious. He probably expected to arrive at the very limits of the known world, even at the ocean itself.[34] So, even if he didn't in fact walk over all the earth, he did endure the anxiety of such a journey. For he hadn't prepared his soul as if he were to come only as far as Palestine, but as if he were to follow everywhere—as if he were even ordered to leave the known world and to go to the outer islands. But even if the vagueness of the command convinced him to expect the opposite, this would also be hard. For him who is about to endure something burdensome, it is much easier to see clearly what he will face and what he should prepare for, than it is to wander everywhere in one's reasoning, now expecting good things here, and now the opposite, and to have confidence in neither of these, but to disbelieve both equally.

CHAPTER 7

These things happened before Abraham came to the promised land. But when he finally reached Palestine and expected to settle there, he found an even greater storm in the harbor. This is no small cause for misery, but even more unbearable than all: when someone thinks that he is set free and that he has come to the very end, and he puts away all care and anxiety, but then he finds yet another beginning of difficulties all over again. For the one who has already prepared for terrible things may bear their introduction easily. But the one who has reclined and released cares from his mind, should things happen again as they did before, he is doubly disturbed and easily

33. Gn 12.1.
34. I.e., the "outward ocean," or, in other words, the ends of the earth.

overcome because it is unexpected and because he had parted from all his zeal and preparation.

What was the storm, then? At that time such a violent famine grasped Palestine that Abraham immediately departed from there and went down to Egypt. And after coming there to find relief from the evil, he again fell into a calamity harsher than famine and was compelled to run a risk with the worst things of all. And it then brought him so much fear that he chose something that is for everyone the most unbearable thing of all: choosing that his own wife be violated. For he then came to such great duress that he even dealt in pretense. What could be more pitiable than this? What state of soul do you think he had, when he was forced to plot such things with his wife? "I know that you are a beautiful woman; therefore, it will happen that when the Egyptians see you, they will ask, 'Is she his wife?' and they will kill me, and they will make you their own. Therefore, say, 'I am his sister,' so that it should go well for me by you, and my soul will live because of you."[35]

The one who uttered these words was the same one who, for the sake of God, had given up his country, home, friends, kindred, and everything else pertaining to his household, who endured so much humiliation and toil on the journey for so long. Yet he said nothing like, "God has abandoned me, rejected me, and expelled me from his characteristic providence." But he bore all things nobly and faithfully, even what he should have been angered at most of all: when his wife was violated with great violence. He did everything lest the offense become manifest. And it is impossible to put into words how much despondency and misery this held for him. Whoever has a wife (460) and falls into suspicion of rivalry knows this. Solomon thus testifies to this emotion and says, "Full of jealousy is the anger of her husband; it will not spare in the day of judgment, nor will it exchange enmity for a ransom; nor will it be discharged by any bribes."[36] And again, "Love is as powerful as death, jealousy as hard as Hades."[37] But if he who

35. Gn 12.11–13.
36. Prv 6.34–35.
37. Song 8.6.

is jealous is so consumed, what could be more pitiful than the man who is overcome by such evils that he is even compelled to persuade his wife to be violated (which needed to be done to be kept from danger), so that the adulterer might readily enjoy his wife?

And when these evils came to an end, other terrible things were again produced, and the enemy received the same famine. For I am now passing over the quarrel between the shepherds and the distribution of land to his nephew. If we were to scrutinize these events at another time, they would be sufficient to cast one into much despondency. For when Abraham extended the offer to the one[38] whom he saved and who became the master of so many goods—and to whom it was necessary to give up all of this to show honor to his shepherds—he was greedy for the more favorable parts of the land and left the more desolate parts to Abraham. Who could easily bear not the loss, but being dishonored after having been honored, and the acquisition of something worse, which seems to be more difficult than any loss? Nevertheless, I now pass over all this. For our discussion concerns the patriarch, not one of the multitude.[39]

CHAPTER 8

Indeed, the war with the Persians succeeded that famine and forced him to go to battle against them—not from the very beginning, when both the parts yet remained unharmed, but only after everyone had turned to flight, the enemies had prevailed, and no one was able to withstand them, when some were utterly destroyed, some hid, and some were enslaved by them. Nevertheless, none of these things persuaded Abraham to stay home. Rather, since he was struck by excessive despondency at what happened, he went away and participated in their evils, and threw himself to a foreseeable death. For drawing up in battle array against so great an army, with only three hundred household slaves and a few more, he reckoned

38. I.e., Lot.
39. Again, Lot.

it would result in nothing other than his captivity and punishment, and he was prepared for myriad deaths. So he went out so that he might also enjoy the benefit of barbarian cruelty.[40]

But after he had been rescued by the philanthropy of God and returned with plunder and with his kindred, he was once again forced to lament his own evils—I mean being childless and having no one to receive his inheritance. Didn't you hear him mourning then, and saying to God, "What will you give to me? But I am perishing childless"?[41] Therefore, consider also that this grief was a recent one. For this very worry and concern entered the righteous man's house along with his bride, or rather even before the bride herself. It is typical for all of us, whenever we begin merely to consider and converse about marriage, to be stung with every concern for this matter. And of all of these concerns, the concern for children is primary, and this fear shakes our souls from that day. But if (461) it happens that after getting married, one or two or three years pass, the feelings of despondency extend, while the feelings of good hope become slackened. And when an even longer time is added, those feelings of good hope finally recede, while despondency overpowers and darkens all the pleasures of the soul and permits it to receive no feeling. Therefore, even if nothing so grievous had happened to him, nevertheless everything had occurred in his mind. And having the despondency of being childless accompanying everything that happened was sufficient to shade over and cast down all joy. For the promise of God came then—in extreme old age, when the things of nature had been despaired of. And for all the previous time, which was so very long, he endured suffering and mourning. He saw his wealth grow so much that he grieved all the more, since there was no one who would receive it.

What do you think he suffered when he heard, "Your seed will be sojourners in a land not their own, and they will enslave and do evil to them, and they will humiliate them for four hundred years"?[42] And now his wife orders him to take

40. This paragraph is a summary of Gn 14.
41. Gn 15.2.
42. Gn 15.13.

her handmaiden. But then, when Abraham takes her, his wife accuses and blames him, calls God against him, and forces him to cast out the one who shared their marriage bed, when she was finally about to bear a child for him. Who would not be thrown into the utmost despondency? Even if these things now seem to someone to be insignificant, let him reckon that entire households are upset because of this and then let him be amazed at the righteous man. For even if he bore it nobly through the fear of God, he was nevertheless a human being and was stung and pained by all these things. And the female slave came back again to the master's household and bore the illegitimate child to him, and Abraham became a father after all that time. And although he did have something pleasant, he had a greater despondency. For the illegitimate child reminded him of the legitimate child and brought about an even greater desire for the thing. For he believed that the promise, "this one will not be your heir, but he who comes out from you,"[43] was spoken about Ishmael, as God had said nothing about Sarah.

But when he finally received a clearer promise about Isaac, and the time of the birth was determined, before he could again find pleasure in these hopes, the misfortunes of the Sodomites poured out a great fog of despondency. For it is clear to all from the words themselves and the supplication that he offered to God on their behalf that the event disturbed the righteous man in no ordinary manner. When, however, he saw that most horrendous rain falling and everything suddenly becoming dust and ashes, there was nothing left in him. For if we are taken aback and we fall down from despondency and fear when from a distance we see homes burned, what wouldn't that man have suffered when he saw whole cities and regions, along with their inhabitants, in no typical conflagration but being burnt up in a strange and fearful way?

Doesn't it seem to you that the sufferings of the righteous man imitated the constant succession of the waves of the sea? For just as in that case, when the first waves have not yet dis-

---

43. Gn 15.4.

appeared, the next ones peak, so this also always happened in this righteous man's life. For while the evils were still flourishing in Sodom, the king of Gerar attempted with Sarah the same deed that Pharaoh had done. Again, the woman was forced (462) to play the part of a pitiful actor, and the violation would have come to an act, except that again God prevented it.

For as soon as the child,[44] the wife, and all the household celebrated the birth of the child, the righteous man alone was forced to suffer and despond in the midst of such great pleasure, being forced to throw out the concubine with the child. For even if Ishmael was an illegitimate child and born of a concubine, the tyranny of nature was not at all diminished because of her devalued status, nor did the low birth of his mother weaken the force of Abraham's fatherly affections. One can learn this from the Bible itself. For the same steadfast and brave man who permitted himself to slaughter his firstborn with his own hands suffered when his wife ordered him to do these things. And he wouldn't have borne it or been persuaded by Sarah—who then exercised much freedom of speech and spoke to him—unless the fear of God had bent him exceedingly low. So, when you hear that he sent them away as God commanded, do not believe that his pain was relieved (for this was impossible), but be amazed at his exceedingly great obedience—that even when he was moved to pity by sympathy, he didn't speak against God but sent away the child, along with his mother, not seeing where she journeyed. But he endured and held fast, even while being pained. For he was not stronger than nature.

CHAPTER 9

And he suffered this same thing in the case of his legitimate child. Don't let anyone say that he was neither pained, nor endured fatherly experiences, nor, because you want to show that he philosophized beyond measure, let this main point rob him of praises. For we suffer and are cast down—

44. Ishmael.

and even often cry—if we unexpectedly see in the marketplace those who are caught up in shameful things, who have enjoyed this life for a long time, who are unknown and unseen to us, being led away to their death. When Abraham was ordered to sacrifice and burn up with his own hands his legitimate and firstborn son, who was born to him against hope, after so much time, in extreme old age (for these things excite an even greater flame), who was still young, did Abraham suffer nothing human? What could be more ridiculous than saying this?

For if he were made of stone, iron, or adamant itself, wouldn't he be bent and broken because of the age of his son (for he was still in the bloom of youth), because of the significance of his words, and because of the piety of his soul? He asked his father, saying, "Here are the wood and the fire; where is the sheep?"[45] He heard that "God will see for himself the sheep for the whole burnt offering, O child,"[46] and he was no longer curious. He saw his father binding him, and he did not recoil. He was placed upon the wood and did not leap off. He saw the dagger being lifted against him and was not disturbed. What could be more pious than this soul?

Therefore, will anyone now dare to say that Abraham suffered nothing on account of all this? For if he were about to sacrifice an enemy and a hostile—or even a beast—would he do this without pain? This is not so—not so. And lest you convict the righteous man of such great cruelty: he also suffered and was cut through. He said, "God (463) will see for himself the sheep for the whole burnt offering, child."[47] How much sympathy do you think these words have? But he nevertheless kept back and pressed down the pain, and did everything with as much willingness as those who are seized by none of these impediments.

Therefore, when he had sacrificed him (for he really did sacrifice him with eagerness),[48] he returned him safe and

---

45. Gn 22.7.
46. Gn 22.8.
47. Ibid.
48. προθυμία. Or "willingly." See also *Scand.* 10.12.

sound to his mother. And once she received him back, before having had her fill of her son, she reached the end of her life. This grieved Abraham in no small measure. For although they were together for a long time, that wasn't enough to persuade him to bear the misfortune lightly. In fact, this very thing brought him more despondency. For I consider those who have lived together for a long time, and who have given us a great proof of their friendship and virtue, to be the greatest of all. The patriarch himself makes clear that this is the case when he grieves and mourns her.

What should be said about his concern for his child, his wife, his brethren, and everything else? If someone wanted to scrutinize this with accuracy, he would see that the righteous man's life was even harder than now shown and full of many worries. And Scripture, since it mentions only the more important things for us to scrutinize, passes over all the other things that usually happen in a household every day, where there are a multitude of slaves, husband, wife, and children, and where attention must be given to many affairs.

"Yes," you may say, "but enduring all those things for God brought to him the greatest consolation for each of these griefs." So will it also console you now! For he who allowed this trial to come upon you is no one but God. If those evil demons wouldn't dare to rush upon swine except when he allowed them to do so,[49] how much more upon your honorable soul. Therefore, just as bearing everything nobly and thankfully brought a great reward to that man, such will it also bring to you—so long as you are neither annoyed nor indignant, but for everything give thanks to God, who loves humanity. And when blessed Job suffered what he suffered and God allowed it, the suffering brought him not only crowns, but withstanding everything nobly also brought him terrors. And we are all amazed at him, not because the devil robbed him of everything, but because in all these things he did not sin, not even with his lips.[50]

49. Mk 5.1–17 and par.
50. Jb 1.22.

CHAPTER 10

When I mentioned Job, it made me want to set out a discussion of his long laments and the excess of his sufferings. So as not to make the discussion too long, however, I return to Isaac. But if you do want to learn accurately about Job, take his book in your hands and peer into the abyss of his misfortunes. You will find much consolation for yourself in them. For even if the righteous man is much better than we are, he also stood prepared for a much greater performance. For at that time the evil one raged against him with great violence. But triumphs are judged not by the measure of the trials, but by the power of what is done. So, even if he who now contends is inferior,[51] nothing will be able to keep you from the crowns. For the one who offered two talents brought no less than the one who displayed five. Why? Because even if the payment is not the same (464), yet the readiness[52] is the same, for which reason each obtained the same honor, hearing, "Enter into the joy of your Lord."[53]

What about Isaac, then? He was neither sent on a long journey as his father was, nor forced to give up his own land as he did, but he did himself endure the chief of evils: the fear of being childless. And just after he prayed and relaxed this terror, another fear overtook him, greater than the first. For trembling on account of being childless is not the same as trembling for the root itself. For his wife was so broken up with anguish that he endured a life more bitter than any death. Hear the same woman[54] saying, "If this is about to happen to me, why am I alive?"[55] And when he received the trial of famine, even if he didn't himself go down to Egypt, he also endured the same things as his father almost suffered there, and ran the same risk with his wife. And whereas all those who dwelt near had high regard for his father, they drove him off like an

---

51. I.e., Stagirius's demon is inferior to the Satan, with whom Job contends.
52. προθυμία.
53. Mt 25.21.
54. I.e., Rebecca.
55. A conflation of Gn 25.22 and Gn 27.46.

enemy and a hostile, and they didn't leave him alone to enjoy the benefits from his own toil, but brought him much anguish and arrogantly reveled in his hardships.[56] But as soon as he acquired these as friends and saw his children coming of age, then, at the very time when he expected to find much consolation and to be well taken care of in his old age, he fell into the utmost despondency. First, against his father's advice, the elder son took a wife from the foreigners and distressed him exceedingly both by this itself and by introducing fighting and war into the household. For those women[57] exposed them to myriad evils, all of which Scripture refrains from discussing, but through one word hints at everything, saying, "They quarreled with Rebecca."[58] I leave it to those who have houses and children and who are already married, to know what was said. For more than anyone else, these know accurately what sort of evil it is for one's mother-in-law and one's wife to be contentiously disposed, and all the more when they both live in a single house. This terror was therefore continuous: what happened in these times—the blindness of the eyes, which only those who suffer such evil know—and, after this—his failure to bless the child, by which his soul was so stung that he cried out more bitterly than the one who endured the deception,[59] and even defended himself to Esau. For it doesn't say that he was wronged knowingly, but that he was deceived. And the events from here on displayed a tragedy upon the stage, and it resembled the drama of the Theban Boys.[60] For here also the elder brother treated his father's age and blindness with contempt, and he cast the younger brother out of the house.

But if Esau didn't kill his brother as the Theban brother did, this is because the mother's wisdom prevented it. For Esau threatened murder and awaited his father's death. But when his mother learned of this and spoke to their father,

---

56. See Gn 26.14–23.
57. "those women": Esau married two non-Hebrew wives; see Gn 26.34.
58. Gn 26.35.
59. That is, Isaac was more upset about Jacob's deception even than Esau.
60. I.e., in Sophocles's three Theban plays and Aeschylus's *Seven against Thebes*.

she snatched Jacob from his hands, and they were forced (465) to drive away the one who cared for them and who was so kindly disposed toward them, while they continually kept with them him[61] who conducted a wretched and intolerable life (for Rebecca herself said this).[62] Therefore, after he who was always raised in the house (for it was natural for him to live in the house), and who supervised many matters in the household with his mother, ran away, how much was Rebecca likely to be pained and grieved, constantly recalling the child and observing her husband, who was disposed no better than a corpse through both his old age and his illness? And with how much grief was the old man likely to be troubled both with his own sufferings and when he was also forced to grieve his wife's misfortunes? And when she was about to die and didn't see the child present, weeping, wiping his eyes, shutting his mouth, putting on a grave countenance, and taking care of everything else—which seem to parents to be more bitter than death itself—what didn't she say, what didn't she utter, which would be enough to melt a stone? And when Isaac saw her breathe her last, what sort of soul did he possess—both then and after her death?

CHAPTER 11

Someone who seems to us to be more cheerful than many has just been mentioned. But even without scrutiny Jacob's statement is itself enough to explain his life. For when he was conversing with Pharaoh, he said, "My days have been short and evil, and I haven't reached the days of my fathers."[63] That is, he lived a shorter and more wretched life. But even without this statement his misfortunes are so apparent that none of the multitude are ignorant of them. For although his grandfather[64] was sent on a long sojourn, it was nevertheless God who had given the order, which brought him the greatest conso-

61. I.e., Esau.
62. Gn 27.46.
63. Gn 47.9.
64. Abraham.

lation; but this man was fleeing his brother, who plotted and breathed murder against him. And whereas Abraham never lamented over being supplied with life's necessities, Jacob regarded being furnished with only a cloak and bread as something to be prized and desired.

And after he was rescued and released from the evils of the journey, when he came to his kindred, he who had been raised in so much freedom was forced to work as a slave. Know that in every case slavery is bitter. But when someone is forced by those who are of the same status to endure slavery, when he has never had the experience of the thing but has lived in freedom and luxury for the whole prime of his life, the terror becomes unbearable. He nevertheless bore everything nobly. And you can hear the misery of his work as a shepherd when he relates it: "I would exact for myself thefts in the day and thefts in the night. I have become consumed by the heat of the day and by the frost of the night, and sleep has gone away from my eyes. So it was for me for twenty years."[65] The one who suffered these things was he who had lived a sheltered life, who always lived at home.

And after so much labor and loss for all that time, he endured a bitter deception concerning his wife. Even if he hadn't been in slavery for seven years, and even if he hadn't suffered what he lamented bitterly to his father-in-law,[66] and even if he hadn't longed for a child, what despondency, what disturbance, what indignation would have gripped that blessed man at that time from this alone: being pledged to the better daughter but being given the worse daughter in her place! If it were anyone else, he wouldn't have so easily borne the indignation (466) but would have destroyed all the household of his in-laws and slain himself along with them—or he would have destroyed them together in some other way. But since Jacob was patient and longsuffering, he didn't do this, and neither did he even begin to consider it. And when he was ordered to serve again for another seven years, he readily obeyed—so gentle and mild was he. And if his love for the girl

---

65. Gn 31.39–41.
66. I.e., Laban.

aided the mildness of his ways, you are again speaking about the excess of his despondency! Consider how much pain he endured when he was thus defrauded of the one whom he loved. And when he expected to have her in his family, he was knocked back again to a postponement of seven years—to continuous frost, heat, night watches, and losses. And when he later received this wife and lived a humble and toilsome life on account of his father-in-law, he was so envied—and endured another deception in the case of wages—that he even refuted his father-in-law, saying, "You have defrauded me of ten ewe-lambs."[67] And in addition to the father-in-law, his wives' brothers were more enraged against him even than his father-in-law.

What was hardest of all was that the one he loved, for whom he undertook to serve for twice-seven years, was choked by despondency when she saw her sister bearing children but had no hope of the thing for herself. And she was then carried away into so much anguish by despondency that she accused and complained to her husband, and even threatened death against herself unless she bore children. For she said, "Give me children or else I will die."[68] What then could bring him joy when the one whom he so desired lamented these things, and while her brothers were plotting against him and doing everything so that he might come to the utmost poverty? But if it brings us much despondency when we set aside, without sweat, a dowry for a wife, how could it be that he bore her loss easily when he risked so much to acquire her, with so much toil? Therefore, since he sensed that her brothers cast glances at him and held him in suspicion, escaping their notice he withdrew as a fugitive. What could be more pitiful than this? For after having traveled with fears and dangers both from his own family and from strangers, he was forced to fall into the same pits once again. For he came to his father-in-law when he was fleeing from his brother, but now, having been driven out by his father-in-law, he was forced to fall back onto his brother.

67. Gn 31.41.
68. Gn 30.1.

And he awaited that prophecy which Amos says about the day of the Lord: "As if someone should flee from the face of a lion, and a bear falls upon him; and should he rush into his house, and rest his hand on the wall, and a snake would bite him."[69] But why is it necessary to talk about the trembling that he endured when he was seized by Laban and the afflictions along the way, when so many animals and children were following with him? But when he was about to catch sight of his brother, didn't he suffer in the same way as those who see the head of the Gorgon (which comes from the poets and is fabricated by them)?[70] Didn't he put everything in order as if he were departing to his death? Hear his words and learn about the flame that was stored up in his soul. He says, "Deliver me, O God, from the hand of my brother Esau, for I fear him, lest he come and strike me and the mother along with her children. But you said to me, 'I will make you well.'"[71] How much joy would this fear expel, even if he had been continually in joy for all the previous time? But as it is (467), from that very day when he was about to receive the blessings and he died before his time from fear, his whole life was compounded with misfortunes and plots. For at that time fear so held him that not even after the chance meeting, when his brother acted kindly and philanthropically to him, did he take courage and lay aside the anguish. When Esau suggested that they depart together, Jacob, as if he were about to be released by some beast, thus thought up and concocted a plan for his withdrawal, saying, "My lord, you know that the children are tender, and that my sheep and the cows are in labor. Therefore, if I should drive these too hard, in one day all the animals will die. May my lord proceed before his servant, and I will recover on the way, at leisure for the journey before me, and at my children's pace, until I come to my lord at Seir."[72]

69. Am 5.19.
70. Here Chrysostom apparently feels the need to justify his allusion to a "pagan" reference to "the poets," apparently a reference to Medusa in the Perseus myth. He has no such reservations in mentioning the "Theban boys/brothers," despite his disdain for the theater. See especially Leyerle, *Theatrical Shows*.
71. Gn 32.11.
72. Gn 33.13–14.

And having rested from those dangers for a little, he fell again into another much more difficult fear. For when his daughter was captured, he suffered first by the violation of the child. And while the son of the king consoled him for what happened by promising to take her as a wife in a lawful marriage, and Jacob praised the decision, Levi and those with him annulled the treaty and destroyed the city—men and all—and brought the one who had begotten them into such a state of trembling that he even moved away from there because all were hostile to him. It says, "For Jacob said to Simeon and Levi, 'You have made me hateful, so that I am evil to all those who live in the land, both to the Canaanites and to the Perizzites, and I am smallest in number; and having advanced upon me, they will cut me off, and I and my house will be obliterated.'"[73] And those who dwelt near would have utterly destroyed them all, except that the philanthropy of God held fast their anger, and placed a limit on those evils. For it says, "The fear of God came upon all the cities in their region, and they did not pursue after the sons of Israel."[74]

What about after their deliverance, then? Did he breathe his last? It was at that time that the height of evils came upon him: the death of his beloved, which was both untimely and violent. It says, "Rachel bore a child, and she suffered in childbirth. And it happened, in her difficult labor, that the midwife said to her, 'Take courage, for this is your son.' And it happened, in the giving up of her soul (for she was dying), that she called his name 'Son of my Pain.'"[75] And while Jacob's mourning was yet in full bloom, Reuben added to the despondency by violating the marriage bed of his father. Jacob took this so hard that he even died cursing the child, at the time when parents are most sympathetic to their offspring—and this he did to the one who was first born of all! And this is enough of a reason for no small word of affection. But the violence of despondency nevertheless rejected all these things, and when Jacob called to him, he said, "Reuben is my first-

---

73. Gn 34.30.
74. Gn 35.5.
75. Gn 35.18.

born, my strength, and the beginning of my children; he is hard to bear and stubborn. And having insulted me, may you not boil as water does, for you went up to the bed of your father; you then defiled the couch from which you arose."[76]

And when the son of his beloved wife[77] came to maturity and Jacob expected him to be of some consolation for this sorrow over her, then manifold misfortunes were prepared for him on his account. For (468) the brothers, immersing this son's coat in blood and showing it to their father, brought a complex grief upon him. For he did not mourn the death only but also the manner of the death. And the troubles of his soul were many: that this was the son of his beloved; that he was superior to all the others; that he was most beloved; that in him was the bloom of youth; that he had been sent by Jacob; that he was not in the house, nor upon his bed, nor in the presence of his father, neither speaking nor hearing anything; that it was not the death that is common to all; that while still alive he was torn apart by the savagery of animals; that he didn't find him to collect his remains and deposit him in the earth; that he did not endure these things in youth when he would have been able to bear it, but in extreme old age. Jacob was a spectacle more pitiful to behold than all: his gray hair disgraced with dust, his aged breast stripped of his torn garment, and great lamentations of consolation. For it says, "Jacob rent his garment, put sackcloth upon his loins, and mourned his son for many days. And all his sons and daughters were gathered, and they came to comfort him, and he did not want to be comforted, saying, 'I will go down to Hades mourning my son.'"[78]

And as if he should never cleanse his soul of despondency, when he began to be healed of these blows, a famine thus arrived and seized all the earth. And, at first, he grieved it exceedingly. But when his sons came up from Egypt and brought back some consolation for the evil, they brought it mixed up

76. Gn 49.3–4.
77. Joseph.
78. Gn 37.33–34.

with another grief. And the child's[79] sojourn obliterated the pleasure that came from being delivered from the famine—not only this, but also that they demanded Benjamin, the very one whom Jacob had as his only comfort after his wife went away and his son Joseph was eaten by beasts. And it was not only this that made him cling to Benjamin, but also his age and health. For he said, "My son will not go down with you, for his brother died and he alone is left, and he will happen to become ill on the road on which he travels, and you will bring down my old age with sorrow into Hades."[80] Therefore, for all these reasons, he at first rejected the demand and didn't consent to give him. But when the famine assailed them violently and Jacob sensed the very great need for it, he was exceedingly mournful and said, "What evil have you done to me, announcing to the man whether you have a brother?"[81] And Jacob endured the most painful thing of all, uttering these pitiful words: "There is no Joseph, there is no Simeon, and you will take Benjamin? All these things have happened to me!"[82] He lamented that, after Joseph, they attempted to drag away Simeon and Benjamin from him, and he made plain that he would suffer anything rather than be far from his child. But he was finally overcome and gave him away with his own hands, saying, "Take your brother, arise, and go down to the man. And may my God give you grace in the presence of the man, and may he send away your one brother Simeon and Benjamin. For I have been bereaved (469) as I have been bereaved of my children."[83]

He was so exceedingly overpowered by these many evils—as his innards were being torn apart and his children were reduced little by little—he endured everything in excess of those who were greater than he. For he was gripped by a greater despondency for these things than he was for Joseph. For if the misfortune that has no hope of being set right

---

79. I.e., Simeon, whom Joseph tricked into staying in Egypt.
80. Gn 42.38.
81. Gn 43.6.
82. Gn 42.36.
83. Gn 43.13–14.

brings us extreme despondency, it nevertheless quickly expels this despondency and throws one's reasoning into despair. The misfortune, however, that is still in mid-air doesn't permit the soul to rest and always extends and renews our anguish because of the uncertainty as to what will happen in the future. One may learn this well from blessed David, who mourned while his child still lived, but when it died, he freed himself from mourning. And when his servants were perplexed by this and asked him the reason for it, he provided the same explanation as I just did.[84] Therefore, Jacob likewise feared and trembled more for these reasons.

But the longed-for vision—seeing Joseph—later brought him joy. But what use was this? It was just like limbs burnt thoroughly with fire: even if someone cools them off ten thousand times, it doesn't help. So also nothing was enough to revive Jacob's soul, which was in anguish and consumed with the excessive flame of despondency—and all the more when his senses were probably blurred. This is also what Barzillai was saying when he appealed to David: "How many days of the years of my life will there be for me there, that I should go up with the king to Jerusalem? Today I am eighty years old. Will I know the difference between good and evil? Will your servant taste whatever you eat or whatever you drink? Or should I hear the voice of men or women singing? And why does your servant become a burden to my lord the king?"[85] But why should we have recourse to others,[86] when it is possible to hear from the very one who had suffered these things? For after seeing his son, it says that he[87] was asked by the Pharaoh about his life. And he said, "My days have been short and evil, and I haven't reached the days of my fathers."[88] Thus he ever had the memory of what had happened raging in his soul.

---

84. 2 Sm 12.21–23.
85. 2 Sm 19.34–35.
86. I.e., Barzillai.
87. I.e., Jacob.
88. Gn 47.9.

CHAPTER 12

But whom didn't this bright and distinguished son, Joseph, eclipse with his misfortunes? For while his father had only one brother who plotted against him, Joseph had many more. And while Jacob was raised from his early youth in great abundance and ease, Joseph was forced to bear the misery of a journey to a foreign land when he was still a child. And Jacob's mother was present to relieve him of Esau's plot; but Joseph, when he was still young and could really have used his mother, lacked her help. In addition to this, Esau distressed Jacob only to the point of threatening him; but Joseph's brothers brought the plot to action, and before the plot they envied him and complained about him, and finally brought it to completion. What could be harder than this—always having enemies living with him? "For they even brought an evil accusation against him,"[89] "and seeing that his father loved him more than his other sons, they hated him and were not able to speak anything peaceable to him."[90] For neither what happened under the traders (470) nor what happened under the eunuch could be said to be so evil. For they treated him much more philanthropically than his brothers did!

The storm of misfortunes, however, did not then become milder. A violent wind fell upon him again and sunk him. One might assume that I am talking about the mistress's plot. But before that I will mention another very difficult thing. For it is terrible—truly terrible—for a free and wellborn child who was so unaccustomed to such necessity to be falsely accused and condemned for such things, and to live in prison for so much time. But I think that much more difficult than all these was the storm that came from his age. For if he spat upon her love when he was irritated by no lust at all, I wouldn't offer him much praise. Nor would I be amazed at the man who believes in Christ. For he says that it is not those who are eunuchs by nature, but those who "make themselves eunuchs for

---

89. Gn 37.2. MT has "He [Joseph] brought an evil accusation against them."
90. Gn 37.4.

the kingdom of heaven,"[91] who are deemed worthy. But if he wasn't this kind of eunuch, what kind of victory is extolled? What did he receive the crown for? What is he extolled for overcoming if there is no one wrestling with him and attempting to overthrow him? We don't praise for their self-control those who don't have intercourse with irrational beasts, because lust for that union doesn't lie in our nature. If, however, at that time this fire wasn't troubling that blessed man, for what reason are we amazed at him for his self-control? But if the licentious woman set upon the youth at the time when the flame rises highest of all—for he was, after all, twenty years old—and when its tyranny is irresistible and nothing can increase it, and if she added as much strength to the flame from her deceptions and ornaments as she had from nature, how could someone tell of the soul's storm and disturbance and anguish, with nature and age disturbing him from within, and with the contrivances of the Egyptian woman assaulting him from without—and these not for only one or two days, but for a long time? For I imagine that he then trembled not only for himself, but that he also suffered for the sake of her who pressed him to come to so high a precipice. This is clear to us from the fact that he responded to her with much gentleness. For if he wanted, he could have spoken to her in a more forceful and bolder way, since she bore all things easily through love. But he neither spoke nor even thought any such thing, but, having stirred up pious thoughts—through which he thought only to shame her—he added nothing more. For he said, "Behold, my lord knows nothing of what happens in his house because of me, and all that is his he has given into my hand, and he doesn't withhold anything from me in this house, neither would he withhold anything save yourself, because you are his wife. And how will I do this evil word, and will I sin before God?"[92] And after such great graciousness and a display of self-control, he was accused falsely, and God allowed it. He was bound, and he neither refuted the plot nor the woman's unjust slander.

91. Mt 19.12.
92. Gn 39.8–9.

For God wanted there to be many rewards and more illustrious crowns for him, and it is for this same reason that when the slaves of the king were released, Joseph still remained within. And don't tell me about the philanthropy of the jailer, but instead scrutinize Joseph's words, and you will see the pain of his (471) soul. After the interpretation of the dream, he spoke to the cupbearer: "But remember me, when it goes well for you; and do an act of mercy to me, and remember me to Pharaoh and lead me out of this stronghold, for I was stolen by theft out of the land of the Hebrews, and up to this point I have done nothing, but they threw me into the house of this pit."[93] Even if he bore the imprisonment easily, living together with such men as grave-robbers, thieves, parricides, adulterers, murderers (for this dwelling was full of all these kinds of people) was still more grievous for him than everything else. It is not only this that grieved and afflicted him, but also the sight of many who were wasting away there in vain and without reason. Nevertheless, the household slave,[94] whom you mourn over even now, was set free from his chains, while the free man continued still to be miserable. And if someone were to mention the kingdom,[95] that would only remind me of the flood of worries, sleepless nights, and any number of things that, for those who embrace the quiet and simple life, are most certainly (472) unpleasant.

And besides this, even if something good happened to those men, yet it was when the kingdom had not yet been brought to light, nor when the promise of the future was apparent. But now, when so many good things are laid before us and the thing is clear to everyone, tell me, will someone be pained if he enjoys nothing good in the present life? And will he think that anything that happens here is good when he sees *those* things later? What could be more miserable than the soul that, when it expects to depart a little later to heaven, seeks after indulgence here and joy that is no better than

---

93. Gn 40.14–15.
94. The chief cupbearer of Gn 40.
95. Referring to the kingdom over which Joseph ruled, or Joseph's sovereignty over the kingdom.

shadows? For it says, "Vanity of vanities, all is vanity."[96] And if he who, more than all men, received the experience of the pleasure of this life[97] brought out such a statement against it, how much more is it necessary for us to be disposed and to think in this way—we who have nothing in common with the earth, but who are enrolled in the city above, and who are also ordered to transfer our mind there?[98]

96. Eccl 1.2.
97. I.e., Solomon.
98. See Phil 3.20.

BOOK III

*His Consolation to Stagirius,
concerning despondency*

WHAT HAS BEEN said, then, is enough even to quench the flame of despondency and to persuade the soul to be easily disposed. But I have decided also to deliver another discourse to you, having already spoken the first one, so that consolation might come to you in abundance. For tell me: if someone were summoning you to rule over a kingdom—one on the earth—and then, before entering the city and receiving the crown, you were about to lodge in an inn in which there are mud, smoke, the hubbub of travelers, disturbance from robbers, distress, and much affliction, would you abandon yourself to those grievous things, or would you not rather despise all these things as if they were nothing? How is it not absurd, then, that when we are about to rule the earth, we are abased by none of the difficulties that befall us, since we exult in the hope of reigning, but, when we are being prepared for the heavens, we fall down and are disturbed at each of the grievous things that happen to us in this way station? The condition of this life itself differs nothing from the way station and the delay at the inn. Wanting to show this, the saints called themselves strangers and sojourners to teach us, by these things, to scorn both the good and the grievous words in the present life and, having been set free from the earth, to bind our whole soul to heaven.

Therefore, let's return now to the saints themselves and move the discussion from Joseph to Moses. For this man, the gentlest of all those upon the earth, was born at a time when his people were treated wickedly. He was separated from those (472) who had begotten him, and for his whole youth didn't know who his parents were, and was raised by barbarian men. What could be harder than this for the Hebrew youth who had a sense of it, even if he seemed to be a king's son countless times. But this wasn't the only terror at that time. He also saw all his compatriots in the direst misfortunes. For how could he, who would suffer neither to live nor to have his name written in God's book apart from the salvation of his compatriots,[1] enjoy the benefit of the good things in the palace, when he saw all of them situated in such a rough sea? For if so much pity for the murder of those children enters into us who come after such a long time and who have no such justification for sympathy for the Jews, what wouldn't that blessed man have suffered, since he was bound with great desire to the whole nation and yet was forced to record with his vision the misfortunes of those who received them and to write about their ancestors who did these evil things?

For I think that he then mourned even more than the parents of those unhappy children. This is clear from what he did afterwards. For when he was unable either to persuade or to compel the man who seemed to be his father to bring that savage and tyrannical order to an end, he himself finally advanced to the very same evils as they had. And right now I am not so shocked by this. Rather, I am greatly astounded at how great the flame of despondency was—guessing from the murder—which he nourished in the meantime. For the one who let his pain burst forth into murder made the earlier things plain from what happened at the end.[2] For he wouldn't have avenged these children with so much violence unless he was consumed by their evils even more than their fathers were. After he took vengeance, then, how long did he keep his soul from that despondency? Was he able, finally, to enjoy (473) that consolation that had come from revenge? In fact, no sooner than the next day did another pain, harder than the first, and a fear so great overtake that blessed man

1. See Ex 32.32.
2. I.e., he makes clear his (earlier) long-lasting flame of despondency through his final action of murder.

that it expelled him from Egypt entirely. Whereas it would be terrible to hear ill from anyone, when it was someone who benefited who did this and who reproached his kindness to him and uttered, "Do you wish to destroy me in the same way as you destroyed the Egyptian yesterday?"[3] then—then indeed—did the offense become unbearable. And so great was the anger that it brought, along with the despondency, that he could have even strangled the one who insulted him. But for Moses there was yet a third thing added to these: the fear of the king, which so ruled over the righteous man's soul that he cast himself out from the country entirely. The son of the king himself thus became a fugitive.

Therefore, if anyone now calls him blessed because he was raised in palaces, let him remember that abundance, and he will see that this became a reason for the righteous man's infinite despondency and discontent. For it's not the same for someone raised in a common household who has endured many labors, sojourns, and miseries to suffer long wanderings and to endure evils in foreign places—and coming to no brief experience of these—as it is for someone who has remained all his time in luxury to suffer the same thing. For fleeing will seem more difficult to the latter than to the former, if in fact it happens that he comes to this necessity—which then indeed came about for Moses. And after he became a fugitive, he was brought down to the house of an idolatrous and foreign man. This is no small reason for despondency: to be a stranger for so long a time in the house of one who was a priest to the demons. But being entrusted with the care of his flocks, Moses thus remained with him for forty years.

But if this seems to anyone to be nothing terrible, let's scrutinize those who sojourn and hide not because of fear and terror, but who are willingly separated from their homes for a short time: how distraught they are, how unable to endure, and how good they reckon the return to be! But when both fear and a miserable life are added to this, these heavy and burdensome things appear lighter than the most pleasant return.

3. Ex 2.14.

See the complexity of the misfortune. Do not merely hear, "he tended the sheep,"[4] but remember now the words of Jacob, when he lamented bitterly to his father-in-law, saying, "I would exact from myself thefts in the day and thefts in the night. I have become consumed by the heat of the day and by the frost of the night, and sleep has gone away from my eyes. So it was for me for twenty years."[5] For it is likely that all these same things happened to him for many years and with much severity, so much more desolate was this region than that, even if Moses didn't mourn over these things (nor would that other blessed man have said this except that he came to much need of the thing and was forced to come to these words by his father-in-law's insolence). Therefore, while the estrangement itself, of its own accord, was enough to bring low the man who was sojourning only because of necessity—for they say that an enslaved man, when he is estranged from his own country, is as a bird when it flies away from its nest—he then, additionally, had no confidence in his own safety; but just as some coarse household slave who has escaped his master is always afraid and fears lest he be caught, so blessed Moses also lived in continual fear. This is clear from the fact that when God ordered him to go back after so long a time, he withdrew and hesitated, even after hearing that "the one who sought his soul has died."[6]

CHAPTER 2

But when he was persuaded and departed, and he was forced to leave behind his wife and children,[7] there were again censures, rebukes, and threats from the one who then ruled Egypt, as well as accusations and curses from the very ones whom he was benefiting. Thus, the one said, "Why, Moses and Aaron,

---

4. Ex 3.1.
5. Gn 31.39–41.
6. Ex 4.19.
7. Chrysostom here perhaps takes the singular, "he turned to Egypt," to mean that he did not take his wife and children, whom he had "put on donkeys" (Ex 4.20), despite the fact that soon after this Zipporah is with Moses, circumcising Moses's son (4.25).

do you lead the people away from their works? Each of you, depart to your works,"[8] while the Israelites said, "Behold, let God judge you, for you have made our odor loathsome before Pharaoh and before his servants, to put a broad sword into his hands to kill us."[9] These things were thus grievous and burdensome. But the one that was heaviest of all was that after he had introduced and promised countless good things—freedom and deliverance from the evils that hung over them—he seemed to be a liar. For not only was the burden of the slavery that hung over them not lightened, but it was made even more difficult. And the one who was expected to be deliverer of the whole nation—and who promised as much—seemed to be the cause of the tortures and scourges: both enemy and destroyer. Who wouldn't easily be consumed by despondency when he was promised release from such great evils, but after the promise saw the addition of other more difficult ones?

While he was despondent, then (as it is fitting for someone who hears and sees these things to despond), he was not diverted because of the emotion[10] but remained unwavering, even when events didn't come together according to the promises and even contradicted them. He approached God and spoke about this, bitterly lamenting many things. He said, "Lord, why did you harm your people, and why did you send me? From the time I approached Pharaoh to speak in your name, he harmed this people, and you did not rescue your people."[11] Thus grieving over these things and again hearing the same thing that he had heard before, he again reported the same thing to the Israelites. They didn't, however, allow their souls to be commanded, because of their labor and despondency. For it says, "They did not listen to Moses on account of their despondency and from the hard works."[12]

And this afflicted him not just once in a while. But as it happened at the time of the signs, he was frequently ridiculed

8. Ex 5.4.
9. Ex 5.21.
10. πάθος.
11. Ex 5.22–23.
12. Ex 6.9. LXX has not ἀθυμία, but ὀλιγοψυχία.

by Pharaoh and bore even this mockery nobly. But when he was released from Egypt and he along with the Jews finally took heart, before he really breathed easily, he was seized by the same fear as before—or rather a fear much greater than before. It hadn't yet been three whole days,[13] and he saw all the barbarians with weapons standing next to them. And he suffered in the same way as runaway slaves in a foreign country, whose eyes suddenly alight upon their masters. Or it is as if the Israelites themselves are enjoying pleasant dreams, and, when they are imagining this very escape, they then wake up and find themselves once again in Egypt and in the same evils. Or rather, I don't know which one I should say they considered a dream: their three days of freedom or that present horrible and fearful vision. So much gloom of despondency was dispersed over everyone's eyes! But Moses (475) was seized by a greater darkness. For he feared not only the Egyptians—just as the rest of the Israelites did—but also, along with them, the Israelites. For both eventually regarded him as a cheat and a rogue: those who mocked and insulted and those who were stung and desponding.

But why is it necessary to testify to the man's despondency with these examples, since it is possible to learn well all his pain from the voice borne from above? For when Moses was silent and didn't venture to move his lips, God said to him, "Why do you call to me?"[14] displaying to us by this one utterance the disturbance of Moses's soul.

CHAPTER 3

And when this fear was eased, yet greater terrors arose. All along the journey those whom he governed and who enjoyed the benefits of myriad good things on his account treated him more grievously than did the Egyptians and Pharaoh. And at first, they pressed upon him violently, throttled him, and

---

13. The Israelites set up camp at three different places: Sukkoth (Ex 12.37); Etham (13.20); and Pi Hahiroth (14.1–2). Chrysostom reasonably assumes that they encamp for only one night at a time.

14. Ex 14.15.

demanded of him the meat that was in Egypt, taking no delight in the present, but seeking what they had before—and this was more burdensome than all. For what could he have suffered that would be more difficult, if he had been ordered to lead an army of insane and delirious men? But that blessed man nevertheless bore all these things nobly. And if it weren't for the fact that he was disposed tenderly towards them, the terror would have been bearable, and he would have allowed himself to suffer only on account of what had happened to him. But now, because out of his care he was disposed towards them more tenderly than parents, he had yet another reason for despondency on account of their perversity and defilement. For being abused did not harm him as much as the fact that they were the abusers. For while their thanklessness before the abundance of that miraculous food was terrible, some, when they were still in the midst of the miracles, made a show of their evil, lawlessness, and covetousness in gathering the food. And after they advanced a little more, they groaned again—complained again about God's kindnesses. For each of these things that blessed man beat his breast and desponded. For, when they made the calf, they played and luxuriated.[15] And although Moses mourned and grieved and called down curses upon himself for that grievous ruin, nothing at all persuaded him to abandon sympathy for them.

So, when he saw those whom he loved so much becoming ever worse and worse, with what grief—with how many tears—did he live? If someone who has one son can't live when he senses that his son is inclined to evil—even if he himself is the evilest of all—how much more for him who has aquired so many myriads of children in array, and who loved them more than children. For no father should pray to perish with his children when he himself hasn't sinned, as that man did. Indeed, what do you think the one who hates evil and loves good and who had so many children suffered for all of them when he saw them hastening to the precipice of evil, as if by some pact? For, if the whirlpool of that despondency had not darkened him excessively and overthrown his soul from

---

15. See Ex 32.6.

its foundations, he wouldn't have thrown the tablets from his hands and shattered them—though he quickly cured the offense. But tell me, what did he do? For this is also the way of curing: even if he explained away what happened, he himself was nevertheless also full of many tears. And he was not so stony that he suffered nothing when he saw his (476) brothers and compatriots being slaughtered by their own people—and this pitiable slaughter extended to a number of three thousand bodies.[16] For we do the same to our own children when we find them in some terror: while we let them be whipped and flogged, we don't do this without pain—but with no less affliction than they suffer themselves.

CHAPTER 4

So then, when many griefs held him and the camp, yet another agony was added. For God threatened that he would no longer be their general, that he would abandon Moses, and that he would give their leadership to an angel[17]—which for Moses was more unbearable than anything. Therefore, hear what he says to God: "Unless you yourself journey with me, you will not lead me out of here."[18] Do you see how fears give way to fears, and griefs to griefs? And the terrors didn't stop here. But when he persuaded God of this, and he who loves humankind assented and granted the favor, they again surrounded Moses with other pains, provoking the one who was gracious to them and piercing themselves through with the utmost calamities. For, after the much-lamented slaughter, they again offended so much that they incited that fire against themselves, which would have destroyed almost all of them, except that God treated them with so much love.[19]

But for Moses it happened that there was in everything a double despondency: both that those people were destroyed

---

16. Ex 32.28.
17. Ex 33.2–3.
18. Ex 33.15.
19. See Nm 11.1–3. Here his "love" (φιλανθρωπία) seems to refer to his leniency in having the fire only burn up some who were on the edge of the camp.

and that those who were left behind remained uncorrected and gained nothing from their misfortunes. For that death had no effect at all, and those who were left behind remembered the onions and scorned the present things, saying, "What meat will you feed us? For we remember the fish that we ate in Egypt, and the cucumbers, and the melons and the leeks and the onions and the garlic. But now our soul is parched; our eyes [look] to nothing but to manna."[20] Then, no longer bearing their insolence, Moses rejected the leadership and was overcome by despondency, and he prayed for death instead of that bitter life. Indeed, pay close attention to his very words: "And Moses said to God, 'Why do you do evil to your servant, and why have I not found favor before you, that you set the rage of this people against me? Did I take all this people in my womb, or did I bear them, that you say to me, "Take them to your bosom, as a nurse takes an infant, to the land that I swore to give to their fathers"? Where am I to find meat for all this people, that they cry to me, saying, "Give us meat so that we may eat"? I alone will not be able to bear this people; for this word is too heavy for me. But if you do not do this for me, kill and destroy me utterly, if I have found favor before you.'"[21] The one who said these things is the same one who uttered, "And now if you forgive them their sins, forgive them; but if not, blot me out from the book that you wrote."[22] So despondency overthrew him. And parents also often suffer the same thing, being greatly vexed by what their children bring about.

It is clear to us from what he did after this that even after these words his sympathy for them didn't stop. (477) For after the spies' undertaking, when they attempted to destroy him and pelted him with stones, he fled from their hands and again turned to prayer on their behalf, and he entreated God to be merciful to those who wished to destroy him. His love thus pressed upon him more strongly than familial tenderness. Moreover, when the spies died and grief flourished,

20. Nm 11.4–6.
21. Nm 11.11–15.
22. Ex 32.32.

although no time had yet passed, they again devised other causes for his despondency: first, that they didn't uphold the prohibition against war, and second, that they were destroyed by the Amalekites.[23] And even before this battle they were sufficiently consumed with sickness[24] and gluttony: it says, "For he also killed very many among them, while there was still food in their mouth."[25]

After having seen so much death, when his despondency over this had not yet ceased, he was cast again into another grief, and it brought him such distress that he prayed that the lives of those whom he loved and cherished most would be ended by some strange and miraculous death.[26] Thus, some were burned when they unexpectedly caught fire, and others were devoured when a chasm opened.[27] It is not easy to count all those who suffered these things, but they were more than fifteen thousand men.[28]

And when this happened, how do you think their family and friends were disposed towards Moses? And how do you think Moses himself was disposed, when he saw children orphaned, women widowed from these calamities that occurred, sister and brother dying, and that man's sons burned because of some transgression? Each of these is enough to afflict a soul that has not been suffering—and how much more one that has already been overcome by such great evils.

After they conquered the Canaanites and went the long way around, again the Jews groaned and again were destroyed, no longer with sickness as before, nor with fire and a chasm as previously, but with poisonous snake bites that would have destroyed them, unless—again—Moses approached and supplicated God.[29] When they recovered from this destruction and fled the seer's curse, they again flung themselves down the

---

23. See Nm 14.41–45.
24. χολέρα: i.e., a more specific sickness having to do with the digestive tract, and especially with the symptoms of vomiting and diarrhea.
25. Nm 11.33; see Ps 77.30–31.
26. See Nm 16.15; 16.28–30.
27. Nm 16.31–35.
28. See Nm 16.49 and earlier in the chapter.
29. See Nm 21.1–9.

TO STAGIRIUS III 119

most dangerous precipices. After the blessings of Balaam—or rather of God, for the words were not of that man's choosing, but of the power moving him—they fornicated with foreign daughters and were initiated into the rites of Baal-peor. But Moses, having seen such great shame and ridicule, again ordered them to massacre others, saying, "Each of you, kill your neighbor who has been initiated into the rites of Baal-peor."[30] It is just as in the case of a wound: when it has received many incisions and cauteries but is not thereby set in better order, one would again order to incise and cauterize what remained.

But having heard these difficulties, don't think that it was only these things that happened. In fact, I have omitted not a few of the things that occurred: battles, opposition from enemies, long journeys, and his sister's offense,[31] at whose punishment that gentlest man Moses was distressed even more. But nevertheless, even if someone should precisely add everything up, what has been written is not one ten-thousandth part of what happened. For if someone who governs a few (478) slaves in a household has fits of rage and myriad utterances of grief, the one who is forced to be an administrator of so many tens of thousands of people for forty years, and in a desert where there was neither any air nor water, how many events was he forced to endure each day, how many solicitudes, how many despondencies over those who lived and those who died! He even saw all those die whom he led out—save only two men—and those who were born to them, and he was not thought worthy to enter the land of the promise. But he saw it from the peak of Mount Nebo and learned its nature well. But he was not allowed to enjoy its benefit with the rest of the Israelites, and he remained outside and died. For this reason, he himself lamented to the Israelites, saying, "And the Lord God was angry with me about what was spoken by you, and he swore that I would not cross this Jordan and that I would not enter the land that the Lord God is giving to you as an inheritance. For I am dying in this land and am not crossing this Jordan. But you will cross and

30. Nm 25.5.
31. See Nm 12.

will inherit this good land."[32] And the most terrible thing of all that brought him down to Hades with grief was this: he learned beforehand the future evils that the Jews would receive, one after another—idolatry, captivity, unspeakable calamities—so that his soul was worn out not only by the events that he had already seen, but also by what had not yet happened. And as he began to be pained and troubled from his earliest youth, so he also reached the end of his life with the same despondency.

CHAPTER 5

Joshua, who succeeded Moses, enjoyed along with Moses the benefit of everything—that is to say, the painful things. But if he escaped any of it because of his youth, he made up for it after Moses's death. For he rent his garments and sprinkled ashes not only when Moses was living,[33] but also, when Moses died, Joshua came again to the same—or rather to a greater—distress. And not for a short time but for all his days, Joshua lay prostrate upon the ground. Hear his words and his lamentations. It says, "And Joshua tore his garments and fell upon the face of the earth before the Lord until evening—he and the elders of Israel—and they put ashes upon their head and Joshua said, 'I ask, O Lord, why your servant crossed the people over this Jordan to hand them over to the Amorites to destroy us. If only we stayed and dwelt along the Jordan. And what will I say, since Israel turned its neck before its enemy? And when the Canaanite and all who inhabit the land hear, they will encircle us and wear us out from the land.'"[34] And when God heard these things, he showed him the reason for the defeat. And when he learned the reason, Joshua completely destroyed everyone—not only those who sinned but also their relatives and associates, and the multitude of the animals.[35] This disturbed Joshua's soul in no ordinary manner. For if we cannot tolerate seeing strangers be-

32. Dt 4.21–22.
33. See Nm 14.6.
34. Jos 7.6–9.
35. Jos 7.25–26.

ing punished, what wouldn't that man have suffered when he surrounded his compatriots and comrades-in-arms with such evils? And what about the deception of the Gibeonites and the apprehension that came about concerning the tribes that lived at the edge of the Jordan?[36] And what about always going about in (479) wars and battles? And what kind of soul would it have allowed to come to rest? Even if he continued to win, anxiety for those who stayed behind nevertheless disturbed the pleasure that came from the trophies. And the distribution of the spoils was a lot of trouble and brought him many difficulties. Anyone who has distributed property and has given it to brothers or to those from outside the family who become someone's heirs knows this. I don't think it is necessary to speak about the calamities that followed for the people. For it is not now proposed to say whether just anyone led a painful life, but whether it is one of those who is exceedingly well pleasing to God.

CHAPTER 6

Therefore, if it seems good, let's pass by Eli. For he is someone who offends through his children's evil, or rather through his own slothfulness. For he wasn't punished because he had evil children, but because he was more miserly than necessary and didn't defend the laws of God, which were being violated. He even comprehended this himself after that violent threat,[37] and said, "The Lord himself will do what is pleasing before him."[38] Therefore, having passed by this man, we come to Samuel, who was raised in the temple from his youth and was always highly esteemed before God. He demonstrated such great virtue from the earliest age that before he became a man he was reckoned among the most amazing prophets—and this at the time when such things were lacking. For it says, "A vision was not pronounced, and a word was

36. See Jos 9.
37. See 1 Sm 3.17.
38. See 1 Sm 3.12–13; 3.18.

rare."[39] Therefore, this man Samuel, who was born with many tears, was indeed as dismayed and disturbed as is fitting for a right-minded and affectionate student to be, when he saw his teacher carried away to that pitiful death.[40] And after this he was forced continually to lament the misfortunes of the Jews. And his own children, who were unjust and evil and went on to the extremity of evil, grieved him both with this and with not being able to inherit the honor that was afforded to him.[41] And he received, in turn, this despondency; or, rather, he did not receive it *in turn,* for it had never ceased. Instead, the lawlessness of the Israelites' request was added to this, when he descended so far that he was in need of much comfort. Hear, then, what God says to him: "They have not despised you, but me."[42] But even after all this, Samuel nevertheless cared for them so much that he said to them, "And may it not be that I sin by leaving off praying for you."[43]

Therefore, when he saw these people who were so beloved by him acting wickedly, being ruined in wars, and angering God, what pleasure would he have felt? How much time would he have spent without despondency and tears? Even when he appointed Saul as king, pains were continually imposed upon him again and again. For when Saul offered the sacrifice in a way contrary to what was pleasing to God, and when he conquered the Amalekites and spared their king—and this against what was commanded—Samuel was so struck in soul that he no longer saw Saul, but from that time until the end of his days he mourned and wept over him.[44] He was even reproved for the excess of his despondency; for God says, "How long will you mourn over Saul, as I have rejected him?"[45] But if he mourned when these things happened, what about when Saul slaughtered so many priests in vain and for no rea-

---

39. 1 Sm 3.1.
40. See 1 Sm 4.18.
41. See 1 Sm 8.1–5.
42. 1 Sm 8.7.
43. 1 Sm 12.23.
44. See 1 Sm 13.1–15 and 1 Sm 15.1–35.
45. 1 Sm 16.1.

son?[46] Or when Saul came again to destroy the benefactor who had done him no wrong?[47] Or when Samuel saw Saul naked, (480) prophesying and falling over?[48] Or when Samuel heard David lamenting myriad things to him and entreating him?[49]

CHAPTER 7

But when I recall David, I don't know what I should do: whether I should now bring to bear his long and incessant laments, which have been written in the Psalms, or whether, leaving you to read these at your leisure, I should myself review his misfortunes. Indeed, this man David endured many terrible things as a shepherd: battling both inhospitable climates and the savagery of beasts. The former can be seen in what Jacob said, and the latter from what he himself said to Saul about the lion and the bear.[50] And when he gave up that way of life, he fell into the things of war before his time. (I pass over his brothers' jealousy, even if it was excessive—I mean, burdensome.) But after he accomplished that splendid and amazing victory, having taken upon himself single combat, he found, after he had struck down Goliath, an even more violent enemy: Saul, the one whom he had benefited. Saul did not marshal himself against him openly. Rather, assuming the mask of a friend and pretending that David was honored and tenderly cared for, Saul thus arranged for David things that are reserved for enemies. That it is such a great evil to receive as one's due evil things instead of good, hear the blessed prophet constantly lamenting, bearing ill, and saying, "If he repays me evil for good."[51] Therefore, even when no terror was added, this very thing itself was most of all worth much despondency: being the king's general in suspicion and seeming disagreeable to him. And why do I mention that he

46. See 1 Sm 22.6–19.
47. Presumably David. See below.
48. See 1 Sm 19.23–24.
49. See 1 Sm 19.18.
50. See 1 Sm 17.34–37.
51. Ps 34.12; 108.5.

was the king's general? Even if we suffer this from a slave, we are annoyed.

And when plots are devised against the life of a despised man—what life could be more bitter than this? But David nevertheless bore and endured everything. He was present with that man who was thirsty for his blood and waged his wars. But when he went away and situated himself farther from the conflict, this very thing—the distance itself and openness of Saul's enmity—gave him more reason to take courage. But when he was forced to stand against so great a company with his four hundred men, he trembled more than before.[52] Imagine what it was for him to possess neither city nor citadel nor allies nor revenues, and to be forced to do battle with the one who had all these. And, other than the desert and the caves there, he was unable to find anywhere to flee. For even when he took the city called Keilah, he immediately went away from it, because the priest said that God would not save the one who remained there from the hands of Saul.[53] This priest[54] was the same one who had escaped the hands of Saul and brought a report to the king[55] of the tragedy that happened in Nob, when David also burst forth with that bitter exclamation: "For I am the one who is responsible for the souls of the whole of your father's house."[56] Thus, Abiathar's presence with David was always nothing but a reminder of that despondency. For when David looked at Abiathar, he always remembered the destruction of the priests. And remembering their destruction and assigning himself blame for so great (481) a slaughter, he lived a life more wretched than all those who stand condemned. For even if it was nothing other than something that troubled him,[57] thinking that he himself was the slaughterer of so many priests was enough to wound and destroy his soul.

52. See 1 Sm 22.1–2; 23.1–5.
53. See 1 Sm 23.7–13.
54. Abiathar.
55. I.e., David.
56. 1 Sm 22.22.
57. I.e., because it was not true that David was responsible for their death. Rather, it was Saul who ordered the priest Ahimelech (the father of Abiathar) to be slaughtered.

And after he was struck with this thought, which gnawed at his soul more than a moth, both night and day, he also received other successive wounds, one after another. For when Nabal also insulted him through his servants and called him a runaway slave, a deserter, and an insolent slave, the words didn't come without pain.[58] And when he went away to Achish and pretended to be one of those insane people, and he fell down, distorted his eyes, and discharged much foam from his mouth, he wasted away more than those who are truly harassed by demons, when he thought of the necessity to which the one whom he so greatly benefited had brought him.[59]

But when he was briefly at rest,[60] he went onto the side of the enemies. And although he had to make war upon their enemies,[61] the satraps were envious of him and, wanting to discredit him before the king, sent him forth from the army as being useless to them, as well as harmful and a traitor. For it says, "The satraps of the foreigners were angry with him, and they said to Achish, 'Send the man away and let him be turned away to the place to which you have appointed him, and let him not come with us to battle, and let him not become treacherous to the army. And with what will this man be reconciled to his lord, if not with the heads of those men?'"[62] Being struck by these words, David withdrew with much insult and despondency. But when he came home, he found evils so great that he was almost choked with grief. For the terrors that happened at that time were enough to darken his soul even if it had been prepared. But when an unexpected thing was added, and it was contrary to his expectation, it seemed to be twice as bad and was no longer bearable. For he had gone away to rest at home, to find consolation from his children and wives for that despondency. But as soon as he arrived, he heard that they were taken as slaves by their enemies, and he

---

58. See 1 Sm 25.10–11.
59. See 1 Sm 21.10–15.
60. See 1 Sm 27.4.
61. I.e., when he lived among and fought alongside the Philistines: see 1 Sm 27.
62. 1 Sm 29.4.

saw fire, smoke, blood, and corpses. And before he had even grieved and lamented their abduction, those who lived in his city fell upon him more fiercely than beasts, each of them trying to find consolation for his own evils from David's head.[63] It was just as when opposing winds fall upon the sea, and the storm becomes great and fierce from that struggle; so also at that time, when both despondency and fear cut through the righteous man's soul, there was much storm and disturbance, with these alternating emotions[64] continually overpowering and being overpowered.

And once he was able to escape these evils and to recover his wives and all the body of captives, even before he was aware of that victory, he was again struck by a bitter message concerning the slaughter of Jonathan, which so cast down his soul, as can be learned from the lamentations. For it says, "Your love fell upon me like the love of women."[65] Why do I speak of lamentations? For he who cried so much over Jonathan's father—his own enemy and conspirator, who frequently desired to destroy him—what would he have suffered for the one who was present with him in those dangers, who often rescued him from his father's plotting, who had a share in unspeakable things, (482) and who made covenants with him many times over—when David couldn't repay him those benefactions—when he learned that this man had been snatched away from life?

CHAPTER 8

After this suffering flourished, his general[66] surrounded him with another reason for despondency. Joab treacherously killed the one who promised[67] that he would deliver the whole army to David without fatigue and with all ease, and snatched this away before its fulfillment. David felt so much pain at this

63. 1 Sm 30.1–6.
64. πάθος.
65. 2 Sm 1.26.
66. Joab.
67. Abner; see 2 Sm 3.6–21.

slaughter that he even cursed Joab then, and at the very time of the death he charged his own child to exact for himself this price for his bloodthirstiness.[68] The words with which David lamented when he summoned Joab are sufficient to express for us the suffering[69] of his soul. For it says, "The king lifted up his voice and cried out over Abner's grave, and he said, 'If Abner died for the death of Nabal, your hands have not been bound, nor your feet in fetters, nor did you attack as Nabal did. You fell before a son of unrighteousness.'"[70]

And what came after this? Mephibosheth[71] was murdered treacherously. And to the grief that came to David from this—for he again suffered so much at this time that he even destroyed the murderers—there was added the opposition of the lame and the crippled, and it confused him exceedingly.[72] But after he conquered these and other enemies, he returned the Ark with much gladness. But when the Ark was still being returned and everyone was rejoicing, in the midst of the joy an event happened that obscured the pleasure of all and threw the soul of the king into despondency and great fear: the wrath of God immediately struck Uzzah, who wanted to turn around and straighten the Ark, and it laid him down dead. This fear so shook the soul of David that at first he did not dare to return the Ark to himself until learning how it treated Obed-Edom, who then received it.

And after this, when the king of the Ammonites had died, David did the deed of a good and philanthropic man: he sent and consoled the king's son and persuaded him to bear the death of his father lightly. In return for this honor, the king's son shamefully insulted those who departed and thus

---

68. See 2 Sm 23.5–7.

69. Or emotion: πάθος.

70. 2 Sm 3.33–34.

71. Chrysostom appears to have the reading "Mephibosheth," rather than "Ish-Bosheth," in 2 Sm 4.1. This is, per Rahlfs, in keeping with the Lucianic recension (and other Greek recensions), but at odds with MT. In MT, Ish-Bosheth (4.1) is *Saul's* son, but Mephibosheth is *Jonathan's* son (and so Saul's grandson; 2 Sm 4.4; 2 Sm 9.6; 2 Sm 21.7).

72. This seems to be in reference to the Jebusites' taunt in 2 Sm 5.6–8.

sent them away to the king.[73] Does this seem small to you that it struck and cast down his soul? Isn't this exhibited by that war—the war that holds no external reason and extends to such great violence that it should surround him with myriad evils?[74] Therefore, these things are enough, even if someone mixes up myriad pleasures with them,[75] to recount David's life as a life of pains.

But after this such things happened that it was as if the truly grievous things hadn't even begun. For this king's sufferings exceed every myth and every tragedy. Thus, various and successive terrors fell against his house, always hastening to make his bad worse.

Look: Amnon[76] was in love with his sister. And because he longed for her, he violated her; and after he violated her, he hated her and made the violation and intercourse public. And he immediately commanded one of the household slaves to throw her out (483) of the house against her will, and to send her through the marketplace shouting and lamenting. When Absalom learned of this, he called his brothers for a meal, among whom was the violator, and through his household slaves slaughtered Amnon, while he was in the midst of eating and drinking. Then, when someone arose from there without learning what really happened on account of the clamor, he announced to the king that *all* his children had been killed. And David sat mourning the murder of them all, which didn't even happen! But when he heard what really happened, he threatened the servant and said that he would destroy him. And he remained angry with Absalom, who ran away to a foreign place and stayed traveling about for three years, all that time.[77] And he wouldn't have summoned him even then, except that the wisdom of the general threw him into this undertaking against his will. And after he sum-

---

73. See 2 Sm 10.

74. I.e., David himself goes to war against the Ammonites after they insult his servants and fortify themselves against Israel.

75. Perhaps a couched reference to the chapter that follows this episode: David's rape of Bathsheba (2 Sm 11).

76. One of David's sons.

77. See 2 Sm 13. The "general" (below) is Joab.

moned him, this didn't quench the blow to his heart, but for another two years he kept out of his sight. And after all this time he only just consented under the influence of the general[78] and received him into open conversation.[79] But Absalom bore a grudge against him for this, or otherwise longed to be a tyrant, and rose up against his father. And David again returned to wanderings and flights, which he had endured under Saul.

And it showed that this time was much more difficult than the former one. For when David suffered such things formerly, he was a general. But now, after exercising dominion for many years and conquering all his enemies, so to speak, he was forced to depart. And the one who forced him was not some stranger, nor an enemy, but one who came from his belly, as he himself mourned, saying, "coming out from his belly."[80] And previously David was in the prime of life and was able to bear all things nobly. But now, in his old age, when he should have been tended to by that defiled man,[81] he was plotted against and attacked. And the king went forth with a few men on foot, hiding his face and crying. For the war held not only misfortune for him, but also a reason for shame: his son then treated that blessed man so much more insultingly than Saul had that he even violated his father's concubines—and not secretly, but on the rooftop, where all could see.[82] He violated the rules of nature and the laws of intercourse on account of his rage against his father, and, being drunk with folly, while the war was still going on, he dared to make a show of what those who conquer and seize opposing prisoners do. Moreover, when Ziba[83] thus discovered one who was afflicted and afraid, he threw him into much confusion and told lies against his master,[84] saying that he was inclined to tyranny.

78. Joab.
79. For the period of Absalom's isolation from David, see 2 Sm 14.
80. 2 Sm 16.11.
81. Absalom.
82. 2 Sm 16.20–22.
83. A servant.
84. I.e., Mephibosheth; see 2 Sm 16.1–4.

CHAPTER 9

Shimei, a polluted and ungrateful man, received him and threw myriad reproaches and stones at him, with these words: "Go out, man of blood and man of violence. The Lord returned to you all the blood of the house of Saul, in whose place you ruled, and the Lord put the kingdom into the hands of Absalom your son, and he shows you your evil; for you are a man of blood."[85] David wasted away when he heard and suffered these things, as he even made clear from his own laments, but he dared do nothing more. Instead, he said, "Let him curse, for the Lord has spoken to him, so that he may see my humiliation and pay back to me good things in exchange for the curse that happened on this day,"[86] and he allowed him to depart alive. But he waited with Hushai and his party, worrying and fearing what (484) the end would be.

And as these things were reported, the strangest war of all the wars that have ever taken place was waged, and it was rather like an enigma. For David called upon his generals to treat with much care and mercy the one who was the cause of so many evils and who furnished the whole reason for the war—and at whose fall, all terrors were relieved. David constantly recited, "Spare my little boy Absalom!"[87] What could be worse than this dismay? What more pitiable than this helplessness? David was forced to take upon himself a war in which both winning and losing alike were abominable to him. For he desired neither to lose—for in that case he wouldn't have sent out so great an army—nor to prevail over him—for in that case he wouldn't have forbidden the company of war, which was attacking and waging war, from destroying him. And when the war was judged and received the end that God wanted, and that parricide fell, all those who remained were in gladness and joy, but he alone mourned and cried. Shutting himself up, he recalled the child and was unable to endure the fact that he didn't receive death in place of his son. He

---

85. 2 Sm 16.7–8.
86. 2 Sm 16.10–12.
87. 2 Sm 18.5.

said, "Who will give me death in exchange for yours, Absalom, my son?"[88] What could be heard that is more complex than this misfortune? When Absalom destroyed his brother, David hastened to destroy him; but when Absalom raged against him, then David spared his son. And he wouldn't have stopped lamenting the death for a long time, except that Joab entered and showed him the absurdity of the thing, and speaking to him very severely, he stood him up and he prepared him to welcome the army in an appropriate manner.

And his experience of terrors didn't then come to an end. But the soldiers were at first at odds with each other and divided. And when even with much flattery they had only just yielded to the king, they again departed and joined up with Sheba; and again another war, of the remnant left behind from the previous one, broke out afresh. David was disturbed by this. He rallied the soldiers and sent them away with the generals. But even after Joab had turned this battle to victory, he didn't let the pleasure of the victory be free of despondency. For Joab, who had nothing for which he could accuse the fellow-general whom David had put in charge of all his people, but who was simply driven mad with envy, destroyed and killed this general. This disturbed and afflicted the king so much that even when he was dying, he enjoined his child and bound him not to overlook Amasa, who died unprotected.[89]

Even more difficult was that being disposed in this way, he didn't dare to speak the reason for the despondency, because he had already persisted in myriad evils. For after these wars, famine also overtook every land, and when he was looking to find relief from the evil, he was forced to hand over Saul's children to slaughter. For the oracle said this: "The injustice is upon Saul and upon his house; this is because he put the Gibeonites to death."[90] But if anyone recalls how he lamented Saul, he will also know what David suffered when he handed them over to the Gibeonites. But while he was still bearing

88. 2 Sm 18.33.
89. On this paragraph, see 2 Sm 20; on David's charge to his children, see 2 Sm 23.5–7.
90. 2 Sm 21.1.

these things, the misfortunes again advanced further. For after the famine, a plague came, and seventy thousand men fell in the time of half a day,[91] when the king also uttered those pitiable words (485). For he saw the angel drawing his sword and said, "Behold, I the shepherd sinned, and I the shepherd have done evil, and these, the flock, what have they done? Let your hand come upon me and upon my father's house."[92]

It is thus impossible for us to describe all his despondencies with accuracy. For not all of them are recorded. But from his lamentations and mourning it is possible to guess at the magnitude of what was omitted, which is so great that the righteous man never stopped beating his breast and suffering. Why else does it say, "The days of our years: in them are seventy years, and if in strength, eighty years; and most of them are trouble and affliction"?[93] But if you should say that he is remarking not only about his own life, but about the common life, you are saying something more than I myself wish, and you free me from many words, yourself confessing that it isn't possible to find a life that doesn't have many more difficult things than good, whether for David only, or for anyone else. For just as you yourself were saying so nicely—that he considers not only his own experience, but also others' experiences—he thus conveyed this judgment, uttering the same things as the patriarch, with great vehemence. For, what the patriarch declared in part, David later declared in its entirety. For that man said, "Short and evil are my days,"[94] while this man said, "The days of our years: in them are seventy years"—that is for all men—"and most of them are trouble and affliction."[95]

CHAPTER 10

But I leave you at your leisure to go through what I have said with all accuracy, and I will proceed to the rest of the

91. See 2 Sm 24.15.
92. 2 Sm 24.17.
93. Ps 89.10.
94. Gn 47.9.
95. Ps 89.10.

prophets. Although they nowhere provide us with a record of their lives, nevertheless, since they fell into such great difficulty, I think I will be able to show by the excess of the evils that held them fast and from a single word that their whole lives were very painful. First, as was common to all of them, they passed their whole lives being tortured, flogged, sawn in two, stoned, imprisoned, murdered by the sword, clothed in sheepskins and goatskins, going without, afflicted, mortified.[96] And after this they had another increase of despondency more difficult than this: seeing that the evil of those who inflicted these things upon them was advancing. The prophets were harmed more by this than by their own afflictions. One said, "Cursing and deceit and theft and adultery and murder are poured out upon the earth, and they mix blood with blood."[97] The unscrupulousness, complexity, and abundance of evil are clear to us! Another called out again: "Alas! For I have become like one who gathers straw at harvest time, and when for the gleanings there are no clusters in the harvest,"[98] thereby lamenting the scarcity of good men. Another again laments other such things: the goatherd mourned not only his own evils, but he lamented these misfortunes even more than he did his own trials, and he prayed to God saying, "Be merciful, Lord. Who will raise up Jacob? For he is the smallest. Change your mind, Lord, about him."[99] And he didn't thus obtain his request; for he said, "And it will by no means happen, the Lord says."[100] And when Isaiah heard that all the land would be desolate, he didn't want to be comforted, (486) but grieved continually and said, "Leave me alone! I will weep bitterly; you will not prevail in comforting me."[101] For the way of death surpasses every misfortune.

And who could go through the lamentations of Jeremiah, both those that were compiled in private and those that were

96. Cf. Heb 11.35–37.
97. Hos 4.2.
98. Mi 7.1.
99. Am 7.2.
100. Am 7.3.
101. Is 22.4.

spread about everywhere by prophecy—both for the city and for him—without shedding tears? For here he said, "Who will give water to my head, and a spring of tears to my eyes? And I will bewail this people day and night."[102] And there: "Who will give me a remote station in the desert, that I might abandon this people, and depart from them? For all are adulterous."[103] And he complained and shouted, "Alas for me, mother, that you bore a man condemned and judged in all the earth!"[104] And he even cursed the day of his birth, saying, "Cursed is the day on which I was born."[105] And the muddy cistern, afflictions of chains, floggings, plots, and continuous derision disposed him in such a way that he finally despaired. And why, when the city was seized, did he obtain provision and honor from the barbarians? Did he understand these things? Thus, at that time he wrote the bitter lamentations, mourning those who had departed, and he saw terrors that were no less than the previous ones, when those who were left behind from the battle provoked God. For, after he had been promised that all would believe him and not resist, they again went down to Egypt—when the oracle had said to do the opposite!—and they brought the prophet down with them and because of their insolence forced him to predict for them more difficult things than before.[106]

What about Ezekiel? And what about Daniel? Didn't they spend all their time in captivity? The one was punished with hunger and thirst for the crimes of others. And when his wife departed, he was commanded to bear this great misfortune without tears. What could be more grievous than not being allowed to lament your own evils? For I now pass over the fact that he was forced to eat bread placed upon his own dung and to lie upon his one side for one hundred and ninety days[107]— and whatever other things of this sort that he was ordered to

---

102. Jer 9.1.
103. Jer 9.2.
104. Jer 15.10.
105. Jer 20.14.
106. See Jer 42–44.
107. See Ezek 4.

endure. For even if none of the painful things that we omitted and that we just mentioned had happened to him, this alone—that the righteous and pure man was in the midst of enemies, barbarians, and impure men—was harder than every punishment.

Daniel, on the other hand, seems to have enjoyed the benefit of great honor. He went about in palaces and was in power as if he did not live in captivity. But if someone should listen closely to his prayer and observe well his fasting, the alteration of his face, and his constant supplications, and should he really come to know why he did these things, he would see that Daniel, most of all, was in pain and despondency. For not only did the present evils grieve him, but the future things also disturbed him, as he was considered worthy to learn with prophetic eyes what had not yet happened. And although he saw that the Jews had not yet recovered from the earlier servitude, he was forced to foresee another captivity for them. He saw this city not yet constructed (487) and being seized, the Temple being polluted with sacrifices and made desolate, and the whole cult being overthrown. Therefore, he grieved and cried, saying, "The shame of face belongs to us and to our king and to the rulers and to our fathers, as many of us sinned against you, the Lord."[108]

CHAPTER 11

But I don't know how, among the prophets, I have overlooked the soul as high as heaven, who dwelt upon the earth as if in heaven.[109] For he had nothing more than a sheepskin. Who, then, is this great and amazing man—if indeed we must call him a man? After speaking openly to Ahab, after the descent of the fire, after the slaughter of the priests, after the shutting and opening of heaven—according to his wishes both times—after so many mighty triumphs, he was so overcome with fear and with the excess of despondency that he uttered these words: "Take my soul from me, for I am no better

108. Dn 9.8.
109. I.e., Elijah.

than my fathers"[110]—and this from him who had not yet come to his end! Not only this, but departing to the desert, he slept, being overthrown by depression. And his disciple[111] received not only a double spirit of his teacher, but also many more afflictions. Therefore, blessed Paul briefly exhibits these men to us and, counting up their humiliations, says, "Of these the world was not worthy."[112]

And this blessed man was well situated to introduce them to us. For this man, whose appearance alone was enough to comfort, entering after all the others—what despondency and grief wouldn't he eclipse? I don't think it is necessary to speak about the famine, thirst, nakedness, shipwrecks, wearing away in the deserts, fears, dangers, plots, prisons, blows, vigils, the myriad deaths, and as many other things as he endured for the sake of the Gospel. For even if these things furnished some afflictions, they nevertheless also furnished him with pleasures.[113] But when all those in Asia abandoned him, and when the Galatians turned away—the whole highly esteemed nation—and when the Corinthians severed their church into many parts and, having flattered the fornicator, led the church into senselessness, what do you think he suffered? With what great darkness was his soul overpowered? But why would we need reasoned discussions[114] when we can hear the words themselves? For sending a letter to the Corinthians, he said, "From much affliction and anguish of heart I wrote to you through many tears."[115] And again, "Lest in any way God humiliate me when I come, and lest I grieve many of those who sinned in the past who did not repent."[116] And to the Galatians, "My children, for whom I am again in travail, until Christ is formed in you."[117] And he lamented bitterly about the Asians to his disciple.[118]

110. 1 Kgs 19.4.
111. I.e., Elisha.
112. Heb 11.38.
113. See, among others, Rom 5.3; Eph 3.13; Phil 1.12–26.
114. λογισμοί.
115. 2 Cor 2.4.
116. 2 Cor 12.21.
117. Gal 4.19.
118. I.e., to Timothy: see 2 Tm 1.15.

And these things aren't all that distressed him, but the thorn that was given to him also afflicted and oppressed him so much that he frequently prayed to God for relief from it. "Three times"[119] is how often he prayed. And could the one who was struck by the absence of his brother be at all revived? It says, "Upon not finding Titus my brother, I had no relief."[120] And again, in the case of sickness, he suffered this same thing. It says, "For my God had mercy upon him"—he was speaking (488) to the Philippians about Epaphras—"and not only upon him, but also upon me, so that I may not have grief upon grief."[121] And in the case of those who cheated and opposed him, he was horribly depressed and wrote to Timothy and said, "Alexander the metalworker declared many evil things about me. May the Lord repay him according to his works."[122]

Was it possible, then, for him to have even a small cessation from despondency and pain? For what I have mentioned isn't everything that besieged his soul, but others in addition to these continually brought him despondency. He himself again[123] disclosed these things, saying, "Apart from everything else, there is concern for me each day, which is anxiety for all the Church. Who is weak and I am not weak? Who is scandalized and I am not burned?"[124] If, then, he himself was burned in every case of those who are scandalized, it was impossible to extinguish this fire from his soul. For the scandalized did not cease to exist, and they supplied the reason for the fire. Since whole cities and nations have frequently fallen away, it was much more likely that someone or another was always experiencing this, since there were so many churches throughout the known world.

But let's grant, if you wish, with a word, that no one was scandalized, nor ever separated from him, and nothing else

---

119. 2 Cor 12.8.
120. 2 Cor 2.13.
121. Phil 2.27.
122. 2 Tm 4.14.
123. Reading πάλιν for πόλιν.
124. 2 Cor 11.28–29.

grievous happened to him. Even in this case I wouldn't be able to find him free of despondency. Again, I shouldn't need to take any other witness than him who suffered. What does he say? "I was praying to be accursed from Christ for the sake of my brothers, who are my kindred according to the flesh—that is, Israelites."[125] What he is saying is this: "It was more desirable for me to fall into Gehenna than to see the Israelites not believing." This is what "I was praying to be accursed" means.[126] But the one who preferred punishment in Gehenna so that all the Jews could be brought near (it is quite clear that he did not obtain this) lived a more grievous life than those who are punished in Gehenna, since, according to his mindset, it was preferable to the alternative for him.

CHAPTER 12

For each of those I have mentioned, reckon not only the reason why despondency was brought to those men, but also the measure of the grief, and you will see that their pains are greater than yours. For this is what we are now examining: whether they suffered from pain that is more difficult. For it is natural that the measure of despondency be tested not only from the occasion that produces it, but also from their words and from their actions.

Many who merely lose wealth, then, are more pained than Your Love: some who couldn't bear the loss have thrown themselves into the sea, others have fastened nooses, while for others the excess of this despondency has extinguished their eyes. And although losing wealth seems to be less and lighter than your being harassed by the demon, many have nevertheless borne the demon, while they were defeated by the loss of wealth. Do not now examine these things from your own soul, nor, because you laugh at the loss of (489) wealth, think that others are also already so disposed. For the loss of these things has led many to madness and to the utmost harm. For whereas neither of these things can throw down a noble soul,

---

125. Rom 9.3.
126. Ibid.

the soul that is weak and more disposed towards the things of the world is harmed by the loss of wealth more than by the demon.

What do you think? That fearing starvation is not the same as being annoyed for a few days from this illness. For, in your case, all the violence is in a brief span of time, just like a fever, or shuddering, or even when someone knocks you down on the road—or rather, this illness lasts for much less time than those do. But if it overcomes you with its violence, let me continue to show that many of those with fevers are much more out of their minds when they are seized by that fire than those who are harassed by demons. And when there is fear of poverty, which is the lack of necessities, it is like a moth that continually attends to and consumes the soul of those who are impoverished. Why do I mention poverty? For if we wish to count up all the misfortunes of men, and not only ours, you might also laugh at your own laments and wailings. It is impossible for us, then, to mention all—or even the greater part—of them. For we neither know them, nor, if we did know them, would all time be enough to relate them. But, having gathered together a few out of the many, I will leave it to you to guess from these those that are not mentioned, as much as you can.

Remember that most beloved old man—I mean Demophilus—who was from a great and splendid household. This man still had fifteen years of his life remaining, from which time he was disposed no better than a corpse with respect to his activity, except that he trembled constantly, and screamed, and had a clear sense of his own evils. He lived in a state of utmost poverty and had one young slave who served him, who was good and loved his master, but who was not enough to console that misfortune. For the slave was able neither to avert the poverty nor to stop the trembling from the paralysis, but he could only put a morsel into his master's mouth (for his hands were not strong enough for this), guide a cup to his mouth, blow his running nose, and contribute nothing more than this. But when this man still had fifteen years of his life remaining, he was humiliated in this way, as I said. And this reminds me of the one who spent thirty-eight years in this suffering![127]

But consider with me, in addition to this, Aristoxenus the Bithynian. For his body had not been weakened as it had been for the old man Demophilus, but a sickness hung over him, one much more difficult than that man's paralysis. Convulsions and pains, sharper than any pain, pierced through his abdomen worse than a skewer, gnawed more violently than fire, and vexed him each day and night. And in the judgment of those who don't know, they confer upon him the opinion that the ailment is of someone who has been driven mad: thus his pupils are distorted, thus his hands and feet are twisted, and they render him speechless. But his cries and shrieks—for he often cries out after that speechlessness—surpass the loud cries of childbirth. And often those who live far from him who have ailments that trouble them with much insomnia sent and blamed him for their afflictions—that they were becoming (490) worse by this sound. And it affected him not at long intervals, but often in the day *and* often in the night. And now he is in the sixth year from his being handed over to this evil torture, and there is neither a slave present to tend to him, nor a physician to help—the former through poverty and the latter through the fact that the suffering surpassed their skill. For many physicians labored but benefited him not at all. (For so it happened that before this that man had much money.) And indeed, what is more terrible is that not one of his friends wanted to see him in the end, but all abandoned him—even those who had earlier received many kindnesses from him. But even if someone would approach, he would immediately depart. The little room was full of a great stench, since there was no one to take care of it. For one female slave stayed near him, only serving him as much as was appropriate for a woman to do, and one who was alone and was also sustaining herself from the work of her hands.

Then, his evils are more difficult than how many demons!

---

127. See Jn 5.5. Chrysostom demonstrates his high esteem for this man elsewhere—not only in his *Homilies on John,* but also in the opening of his homily on the paralyzed man who was lowered through the roof (*Paralyt.* 1).

For even if none of these things were annoying him, what wouldn't he have suffered when he considered how long he had lain upon his bed, the great cost that threw him into the utmost poverty, the disdain of his friends, the lack of people to attend to him, not knowing whether these terrors would ever stop (which you always grieve), and, even more, believing accurately that while he yet lives and breathes it will never stop? For he says that the intensity of the sickness and its daily worsening are what is terrible to him.

CHAPTER 13

But so that I don't seem tedious to my listeners by tallying up, one by one, those who suffered such things, move on to the one who is charged with the care of the hospital and please introduce yourself to those who are lying there, so that you may see the root of every disease, strange courses of illnesses, and manifold reasons for despondency. From there, go to the prison, and once you learn thoroughly everything that goes on in this dwelling, go to the gateways of the baths, where some lie naked, using filth and straw in place of clothes and houses, oppressed by continual cold, sickness, and famine. They call to those who come past with only their appearance, the trembling of their bodies, and the noise of their chattering teeth, since they are able neither to emit a sound nor to reach out their hands, on account of the fact that they already waste away from so many evils. And don't stop here, but go out to the abode of the poor, which is in front of the city, and then you will see well that the despondency that seems to grip you is now a calm harbor.

For what can one say about men who are consumed little by little by elephantiasis, or women who are devoured by cancer? Both of these illnesses are at once long and incurable. And both of them drive those who have them away from the city, and it is custom that they partake of neither the bath nor the marketplace nor anything else inside the city. This is not the only terror, but also that they have no hope in the provision of necessities. And what about those who are condemned, often vainly and for no reason, to live in the mines? All of these have much greater pain (491) than those who are harassed by demons.

But it isn't surprising if you don't believe this. For we are not accustomed to judge our own affairs and others' affairs to be evil with the same mindset, since we have learned about theirs only by reason and sight, but about ours by experience and sense, and with sympathy with ourselves. Therefore, we think that ours are more unbearable than others', even if they are in fact light and bearable. But if someone, having been freed from all of these things, were to learn well their nature and examine those who fall into them, he would bring to us an impartial reckoning concerning them.

But perhaps you will say this: that all those sufferings only circle around the body, but this sickness strikes the soul and is more difficult than all these others. By the same token, then, we will find that this sickness happens to be much lighter than those. For it doesn't destroy the body, and it troubles the soul for a short time. And those of which we have now taken inventory, they grow in the flesh, but they don't stop there; rather, they pass on to the soul, to torment it constantly and to destroy it with much pain and despondency. As it says, "Just as vinegar is harmful to a wound, so suffering falling upon the body grieves a heart."[128] Therefore, don't say that this is only produced from the body. But, if it doesn't pass every harm and destruction onto the soul, show this to be the case! For although the plague isn't produced from bodies, it does destroy bodies. And the venom of reptiles proceeds from them, but it harms us. So also it happens in the case of these sufferings: while it is produced from the body, it pours out the venom of its evils into our soul.

For more harmful than all demonic activity is the excess of despondency. And when the demon overpowers in whomever it does, it overpowers through the excess of despondency. Should you remove the excess of despondency, no one will suffer anything terrible from the demon. "And how is it possible not to despond?" you may say. But I will ask you, how

---

128. Prv 25.20.

is it *impossible* not to despond? For if adultery and murder, or any other such thing that excludes from the kingdom of heaven,[129] is attempted by you, then despond and grieve! No one is preventing you. But if by the grace of God you have stopped short of all these things a long time ago, why do you vainly beat your breast?

CHAPTER 14

God implanted despondency in our nature not that we might make use of it immoderately and unsuitably in contrary ways, nor that we might pollute ourselves, but that we might gain the greatest things from it. How could it be to our profit? Whenever we receive it in season. But the time for despondency isn't when we *suffer* evilly, but when we *act* evilly. We overturn the order, however, and mix up the occasions: when we do myriad evils, we are not humbled even for a short time, but if we suffer something small from anything whatever, we fall down, become dizzy, and hasten to be set free and depart from this life. For this very reason, then, the thing seems to us to be heavy and burdensome, like anger and lust.[130] And likewise, those who have employed anger and lust neither rightly nor for their fitting purpose have also blamed them.

The same thing happens when medicines are administered by physicians. (492) For when medicines are applied to conditions to which they don't correspond and for which they aren't prepared, but for some condition or another, not only do they not release the sick person from his pain, but they even further aggravate the sickness. Therefore, despondency also does this, and fittingly. For, being a bitter and corrosive medicine—someone might even say a purgative for the evil that is within us—when it is offered to a lazy and luxurious soul that has a great heap of sins, it greatly benefits the recipient. But when it is offered to a soul that is contending, striving, toiling,

---

129. See Gal 5.13–19; Eph 5.5; 1 Cor 5.9–10.
130. These are θυμός and ἐπιθυμία: famously Plato's two lower parts of the soul (below λόγος or νοῦς). Here Chrysostom is harnessing them to demonstrate the power of another θυμ* word, ἀθυμία.

being anxious, and suffering evilly, it is of no use and even harms that soul very greatly, making it weaker and more easily destroyed. For this reason, Paul, when he was writing, said to those who endure and who struggle, "Rejoice in the Lord always; again I say, rejoice."[131] And to those who are relaxed and who have much excess,[132] he said, "And you have been puffed up, and you have not instead mourned."[133] Let the one who is pampered in the fatness of his sins wither and waste away with this medicine! But the one who is in good condition and who keeps himself in a suitable state, why should he destroy the good habit through despondency? For despondency is so vigorous that even for those who need it, when it is applied for more time than needed, it will bring about great evils. Blessed Paul also feared this, and after he had brought it about, he quickly ordered its removal. And he provided the reason, which I am now speaking about: "lest such a one be swallowed up by excessive grief."[134] And if he knows that it destroys those who stand in need of it when it comes upon them with excess, what will it bring about for those who don't need it at all if they absorb much of it?

"Yes," you may say, "I myself know this, but I don't know how I will repel it and distance my soul from it." And what sort of difficulty is this, my friend? For if it were some lust—even an unnatural bodily desire—or the tyranny of vainglory—the impregnable evil—or some other such passion, you would well be at a loss for the recovery. For while it is by no means impossible for those who are caught by such things, it is nevertheless difficult to escape their snares. Why do you suppose this is? It is because they have pleasure that joins together with them and aids them. And this is the same thread that everywhere encompasses those who are caught. And to begin with, this is difficult to accomplish: to persuade the soul really to desire and want to be freed. It closely resembles someone who

---

131. Phil 4.4.
132. φλεγμονή. "Excess" is a metaphorical sense of the word. It is also a medical term, meaning inflammation (hence its correspondence to being "puffed up").
133. 1 Cor 5.2.
134. 2 Cor 2.7.

ought to disregard a scab or an itch but who finds pleasure in the illness and thrusts himself into the condition. But the unpleasantness of this despondency up to this point contributes nothing small for the departure of grief. For the one who is depressed by something will also hasten quickly to reject it.

"Then why should he hasten, if it isn't possible?" Let him not stop hastening, and it will quickly be possible! Consider that if the Christian grieves, he must have only two reasons for despondency: when either he or his neighbor offends God. And since the present pain doesn't have its root in these reasons, you distress (493) yourself in vain.

"And whence is it clear," you may say, "that I'm not paying this penalty for my offenses?" It is very clear, except that I haven't so far strongly maintained this. But, if you wish, let it not be unclear but—as you said—exceedingly clear that this is a recompense for sins. Tell me, then, do you suffer for this reason? Worthy of much joy indeed is the dissolution of sins here, and not being condemned with the world! For it is necessary for the sufferer to suffer *not* because he is being chastised, but because those sins offend God.[135] For sins keep God far from us and make him an enemy, but what comes from punishment reconciles him to us and prepares him to be favorably disposed and near to us.

And that this sweat and toil is not a repayment for sins, but a cause for crowns and prizes, is clear from this. If, after you lived the earlier part of your life shamefully and prodigally, you had thus transferred yourself to the monks' way of life, this shouldn't thus be suspected. If God applies chastisements for this reason—so that he might turn those who are unyielding to repentance—when repentance is shown, the chastisements are for this reason superfluous indeed! For God is so far from wanting to punish us that he often brings us—who do things worthy of punishment and are greatly lacking in repentance—to our senses with only threats and frightening words.

---

135. Chrysostom seems to mean that we should not despond because of the fact that we suffer, but we should despond on account of our sins. The first is futile and excessive—and this is what is happening with Stagirius. The second is manifestly positive.

You may see this both in the case of Israel and in the case of the city of the Ninevites. For not only did God not apply the punishment, but also, when they demonstrated repentance, he immediately dissolved the threat. For God wants us to suffer no evil, much more even than we want this; and no one could spare himself as much as God would spare us all. So then, when he often terrifies sinners with words and does not punish them, and even sets free from the struggle those who have repented, has he not set you free from the threat—you who demonstrate such great piety and virtue—and does he also hand you over to the actual punishment? How could someone believe this? But, if wickedness had corrupted you (which, as I said, was your life before this), it would be possible for someone to come to this idea. While, however, that life was inferior to the present, this one now is both well-ordered and full of much (494) holiness. So it is everywhere manifest to us that these wrestling bouts are the cause of great crowns.

Therefore, it is necessary, as I said, to stir up both these and other such thoughts, and it is necessary, along with these—and even before these!—to disperse this darkness with prayers and supplications.[136] Blessed David, that amazing and great man, also made use of these medicines continually, and thus repelled the many pains of his afflictions, now *praying* and saying, "The afflictions of my heart are multiplied. Lead me out from my distress."[137] And now, stirring up godly *thoughts:* "Why are you deeply grieved, O my soul, and why do you disturb me? Hope in God, for I will praise him."[138] And again, turning from thoughts to prayers, he says, "Set me free so that I may be refreshed, before I depart and am no more."[139] And from prayers to thoughts: "For what is there for me in heaven, and what have I desired upon the earth, apart from you?"[140]

So also Job contended with his wife, who was advising him

---

136. In what follows, David alternates between these two: thoughts and prayers. The rest of this chapter is concerned with maintaining right prayers and thoughts.
137. Ps 24.17.
138. Ps 41.5; 41.11.
139. Ps 38.14.
140. Ps 72.25.

with satanic words, with *thoughts*. And he rebuked her and said, "Why do you speak like one of the foolish women? If we receive the good things from the hand of the Lord, should we not endure the evil?"[141] And he made use of supplications to God. And blessed Paul assisted those who were in afflictions and trials with both of these,[142] now saying, "If you are without discipline, you are therefore bastards and not sons. For what is a son whom a father does not discipline?"[143] And now praying,[144] he says, "God, who is faithful, will not allow you to be tried more than you are able."[145] And again, "If indeed it is righteous for God to give afflictions to those who afflict you, and relief to you who are afflicted."[146] Therefore, should you yourself desire to use these instruments, you may even fortify yourself well with thoughts from every direction, blockading despondency's access. And with prayers for yourself and for others, making this a strong wall, you will quickly sense the fruits of discipline. For you will profit not only in that you will bear present things nobly, but also, having been trained well by these things, you may finally be unassailable to all life's griefs.

141. Jb 2.10.
142. Prayers and thoughts.
143. Heb 12.8.
144. It is not entirely clear how the following are prayers.
145. 1 Cor 10.13.
146. 2 Thes 1.6–7.

INDICES

GENERAL INDEX

Aaron, 112
Abel, 78–79, 83
Abiathar, 124
Abraham, 21–22, 40, 51–52, 83–93, 96–97
Absalom, 128–31
accuracy. *See akribeia*
Adam, 38, 46–47
adultery, of Stagirius's father, 12, 75
akribeia, 31, 33, 44, 70, 76, 84, 93–95, 132, 141
anger: human, 39, 74, 87, 111, 143; of God, 81, 122. *See also thumos*
Antioch, biblical interpretation of, 23–24
asceticism: in Syria, 4–10; of Stagirius and his colleagues, 30–31, 55

belief. *See* faith
Benjamin, 102
Bible: interpretation of, 19–24; private reading of, 6, 8, 66, 123
body, suffering of, 142

Cain, 38–40, 44–45, 78
captivity, of the Jews, 134–35, 53
chastisement. *See* discipline, punishment
children, of Stagirius's father, 6, 12, 75
choice. *See proairesis*
command, of God, 46–48, 51
creation, 33–34

Daniel, 134–35
David, 123–32

death, nature of, 45
demon-harassment, 25, 30–32, 53, 62, 66, 69–74, 125, 138–42
devil, 42–47, 78
diagnosis, 10–11
dignity, human. *See* honor
discipline, by God, 54–56, 147
dream, of Stagirius, 10–11, 31

emotion, 12–14. *See also pathos*
endurance, 64, 86, 91, 136
envy, 38, 44, 78, 104, 125, 131
epilepsy, 10. *See also* seizures
Esau, 95–96, 99, 104
euthumia. *See* joy
Eve, 20, 46
evil, 15, 18–20, 38–45, 81, 115, 143
Ezekiel, 80, 134

faith, 33, 50, 52, 57, 60; of Abraham, 51
fasting, 8, 30, 66, 71, 135
favor. *See* grace
fear, 31, 37, 40, 43, 47–48, 60, 66, 76, 79–81, 87–91, 94, 98–100, 110–14, 126–27
flood. *See* Noah
freedom, of will. *See proairesis*

Gehenna, 37, 45, 53, 138
genre, 13–14
Gibeonites, 121, 131
gnōmē. *See* mindset
goodness: of God, 12–13, 33, 39, 41, 48–49; of creation, 33; moral, 12, 15

Gorgon, 99
grace, 21, 34, 63–64, 145
Gregory of Nyssa, 17

harm, moral, 42–43, 70, 115, 138–39, 142
haste, 32, 44, 67, 69, 135
hell. *See* Gehenna
hope, 47, 52–53, 89
humility, 36, 53, 63–64, 66
humors, 11, 56

idleness. *See* slothfulness
image, of God, 24
immortality, 34, 36, 47
insanity. *See* madness
Isaac, 51, 90–91, 94–96
Israelites, 80, 113–14, 119–22

Jacob, 95–104
jealousy. *See* envy
Jeremiah, 133–34
Jews, 118–22
Joab, 126–31
Job, 93–94
Joseph, 52, 101–7
Joshua, 120–21
joy, 13, 24, 30, 72, 83, 89, 98–99, 127, 130, 145
judgment: human, 72; divine, 60–63; final, 40, 59–60, 72. *See also* logismos

kindness, divine, 39–40, 48, 115
knowledge, of God, 50, 56

lament. *See* grief
Lazarus, 40–41, 53
logismos, 11–15, 33, 50–52, 69–70
logos. *See* reason
Lot, nephew of Abraham, 22, 88
love, divine, 69. *See also philanthrōpia*
lust, 104–5, 143
luxury. *See* slothfulness

madness (insanity), 30, 46–47, 62–64, 73–74, 125, 138–39
medicine, 55–56, 143–44, 146
Meletius, 4, 6
Mephibosheth, 127
mindset (*gnōmē*), 18–19, 138–39, 142
monks. *See* asceticism
Moses, 22–23, 109–21
murder (kill), 38–39, 95, 97, 110, 126–27

Nabal, 125, 127
nature, human, 34–36
Nemesius of Emesa, 16–17
Noah, 22, 79–83

Palladius of Hierapolis, 3, 6–7
paradise, 35–38
passion. *See pathos*
pathos, 32, 87, 113, 126–27
patience, 54, 97
Paul, the apostle, 37, 56–58
penalty, for sins, 40, 78–79, 145
permission, to suffer, 41–42, 46, 49, 52, 64–67, 78, 93, 147
Pharaoh, 113–14
philanthrōpia, 13, 18, 25, 37–38, 41, 43, 48–49, 93, 116
philosophy, 17–18, 71–72, 74, 91
physician, 56, 140, 143
pleasure (pleasant), 30–32, 89–91, 127–28, 131, 136, 144–45
poverty, 98, 139–41
power: miraculous, 30, 119; of demons, 41–42, 78, 142; of God, 51–52, 62; of human being, 63; of despondency, 89, 102, 126, 136, 142
prayer, 31, 37, 66, 71, 146–47
precision. *See akribeia*
prison, 30, 62, 79–81, 141
proairesis, 18, 42, 47, 72
promises: of God, 34, 37, 48, 51–53, 89–90, 113; of the devil, 35, 47
prophets, 80, 82, 121, 131–36

GENERAL INDEX

providence, 12–13, 15–20, 24–25, 33, 34, 41–50, 56, 66–67, 69, 87
punishment, 19–20, 35, 38–44, 48, 60–62, 72, 79–80, 134–35, 138, 145–46

rape. *See* violation
reading. *See* Bible
reason, *logos*, 7, 14–15, 34, 51
reasoning. *See logismos*
repentance, 11, 35, 38–40, 44–45, 50, 61, 145–46
reputation, 12–15, 66–67, 76–77
resurrection, 60–62
reward, final. *See* judgment, final

salvation, 35–36, 49, 60
Samuel, 121–23
Satan. *See* devil
Saul, 122–24, 129–31
Scripture. *See* Bible
seizures, 10–12, 31. *See also* epilepsy
self-control, 46, 70–71, 105
sense perception, 31–32, 103, 142
shame, 62, 72–77, 81
sickness, 10–11, 29–31, 55, 66, 73, 139–43, 145
silence, 8, 71
Simeon, 100–102
sin, 19–20, 35–36, 38–41, 46–48, 72, 74, 80, 143–45
slavery, 38, 52–54, 64, 66–67, 85, 88–90, 93, 97, 106, 112–14, 119, 124–25, 128, 139–40

slothfulness, 30, 36–37, 42, 44–47, 53, 59, 77, 121, 143
Solomon, 97
starvation, 53–54, 139
Stoicism, 17–19
suicide, 70
sunkatabasis, 18, 24

thanksgiving, 49, 54, 58, 64, 73, 93
Theodoret of Cyrrhus, 8, 17
Theophilus, the Ephesian, 3, 9–10, 31–32
therapy, 13–14
thought. *See logismos*
thumos, 74, 143
tragedy, 95, 124, 128
transgression. *See* sin
trust. *See* faith

vainglory, 64, 144
vigils (sleepless), 7–8, 30, 43, 66, 71, 107, 136
violation, 62, 87–88, 100, 128–29
virtue, 60, 64, 82–83

wealth, 138–39
will. *See proairesis*
wisdom, of God, 49, 56–58

yielding, to God's providence, 23, 57, 64

zeal, 42, 87; of God, 50, 67

INDEX OF HOLY SCRIPTURE

Old Testament

Genesis
1.26: 24, 34
2.20: 34
3.5: 48
3.6: 46
3.17: 36
4.7: 39
4.9: 40
4.12: 39
6.9–12: 79
9.20–23: 81
12.1: 86
12.11–13: 87
14: 89
15.2: 89
15.4: 90
15.13: 89
22.7: 92
22.8: 92
25.22: 94
26.14–23: 95
26.34–35: 95
27.46: 94, 96
30.1: 98
31.39–41: 97, 112
31.41: 98
32.11: 99
33.13–14: 99
34.30: 100
35.5: 100
35.18: 100
37.2: 104
37.4: 104
37.19–20: 52
37.33–34: 101
39.8–9: 105
40.14–15: 106
42.36: 102
42.38: 102
43.6: 102
43.13–14: 102
47.9: 96, 103, 132
49.3–4: 101

Exodus
2.14: 111
3.1: 112
4.19: 112
4.20: 112
4.25: 112
5.4: 113
5.21: 113
5.22–23: 113
6.9: 113
12.37: 114
13.20: 114
14.1–2: 114
14.15: 114
32.6: 36, 115
32.28: 116
32.32: 110, 117
33.2–3: 116
33.15: 116

Numbers
11.1–3: 116
11.4–6: 117
11.11–15: 117
11.33: 118
12: 119
14.6: 120
14.41–45: 118
16.15: 118
16.28–30: 118
16.31–35: 118
16.49: 118
21.1–9: 118
25.5: 119

Deuteronomy
4.21–22: 120
32.15: 36

Joshua
7.6–9: 120
7.25–26: 120
9: 121

1 Samuel
3.1: 122
3.12–13: 121
3.17: 121
3.18: 121
4.18: 122
8.1–5: 122
8.7: 122
12.23: 122
13.1–15: 122
15.1–35: 122
16.1: 122
17.34–37: 123
19.18: 123

INDEX OF HOLY SCRIPTURE

19.23–24: 123
21.10–15: 125
22.1–2: 124
22.6–19: 123
22.22: 124
23.1–5: 124
23.7–13: 124
25.10–11: 125
27: 125
27.4: 125
29.4: 125
30.1–6: 126

2 Samuel
1.26: 126
3.6–21: 126
3.33–34: 127
4.1: 127
4.4: 127
5.6–8: 127
9.6: 127
10: 128
11: 128
12.21–23: 103
13: 128
14: 129
16.1–4: 129
16.7–8: 130
16.10–12: 130
16.11: 129
16.20–22: 129
18.5: 130
18.33: 131
19.34–35: 103
20: 131
21.1: 131
21.7: 127
23.5–7: 127, 131
24.15: 132
24.17: 132

1 Kings
19.4: 136
24.15: 80

2 Chronicles
36.10: 80

Job
1.22: 58, 93
2.10: 147
7.1: 77
21.7: 58
26.14: 58

Psalms (LXX numbering)
24.17: 146
32.15: 63
34.12: 123
35.6: 58
36.6: 57
38.14: 146
41.5: 146
41.11: 146
72.2–5: 58
72.16: 59
72.25: 146
72.27: 54
77.30–31: 118
77.34: 36
89.10: 132
102.11–13: 48
108.5: 123
118.71: 36

Proverbs
3.11: 54
6.34–35: 87
25.20: 142

Sirach
2.1: 53
2.5: 53, 54
33.27: 36

Wisdom of Solomon
1.13: 45

Ecclesiastes
1.2: 107

Song of Songs
8.6: 87

Isaiah
22.4: 133
49.15: 49
55.9: 48

Jeremiah
6.8: 36
9.1: 134
9.2: 134
11.20: 63
12.1: 58, 59
15.10: 134
17.17: 37
20.14: 134
42–44: 134

Lamentations
3.27: 37

Ezekiel
4: 134
11.13: 80
18.23: 45
33.11: 45

Daniel
9.8: 135

Susanna
35: 59

Hosea
4.2: 133
6.6: 50

Amos
5.19: 99
7.2: 133
7.3: 133

Micah
2.6: 82
7.1: 133
7.2: 82

156 INDEX OF HOLY SCRIPTURE

Habakkuk
1.3: 82
1.14: 82

Malachi
4.2 (3.20 LXX): 69

New Testament

Matthew
5.45: 50
7.11: 49
7.14: 37, 78
7.15: 63
9.13: 50
18.14: 50
19.12: 105
19.29: 51
23.27: 102
25.21: 94

Mark
5.1–17: 93
9.35: 71

Luke
5.32: 50
12.7: 50
13.2–4: 61
16.19–31: 53
16.25: 41
18.9–14: 64

John
5.1–15: 23
5.5: 140
16.20: 53
16.33: 37, 77

Romans
2.9: 53
5.3: 136
5.5: 53
9.3: 138
9.20: 58

11.33–36: 56
12.15–16: 30

1 Corinthians
2.9: 48
4.5: 63
5.2: 144
5.5: 41
5.9–10: 143
9.26: 76
10.13: 54, 147
11.9: 34
11.30: 41

2 Corinthians
2.4: 136
2.7: 54, 147
2.13: 137
11.28–29: 137
12.2: 56
12.7–9: 37
12.8: 137
12.21: 136

Galatians
4.19: 136
5.13–19: 143

Ephesians
3.13: 136
5.5: 143
6.12: 43

Philippians
1.12–26: 136
2.27: 137

3.20: 107
4.4: 144

Colossians
2.3: 74
3.2: 70

1 Thessalonians
5.16–18: 50

2 Thessalonians
1.6–7: 147

1 Timothy
2.4: 50

2 Timothy
1.15: 136
3.12: 77
3.14–15: 33
4.7: 76
4.14: 137

Hebrews
4.12: 63
6.18: 51
11.17: 51
11.35–37: 133
11.38: 136
12.8: 147

1 Peter
5.8–9: 43

RECENT VOLUMES IN THE FATHERS
OF THE CHURCH SERIES

ST. JEROME, *Exegetical Epistles, Volume 2,* translated by
Thomas P. Scheck, Volume 148 (2024)

ST. JEROME, *Exegetical Epistles, Volume 1,* translated by
Thomas P. Scheck, Volume 147 (2023)

ORIGEN, *Homilies on Psalms 36–38,* translated by
Michael Heintz, Volume 146 (2023)

ST. EPHREM THE SYRIAN, *Songs for the Fast and Pascha,*
translated by Joshua Falconer, Blake Hartung, and J. Edward Walters,
Volume 145 (2022)

CASSIODORUS, ST. GREGORY THE GREAT, AND
ANONYMOUS GREEK SCHOLIA, *Writings on the Apocalypse,*
translated by Francis X. Gumerlock, Mark DelCogliano,
and T. C. Schmidt, Volume 144 (2022)

*MORALIA ET ASCETICA ARMENIACA: THE OFT-REPEATED
DISCOURSES,* translated by Abraham Terian, Volume 143 (2021)

ORIGEN, *Homilies on Isaiah,* translated by
Elizabeth Ann Dively Lauro, Volume 142 (2021)

ORIGEN, *Homilies on the Psalms: Codex Monacensis Graecus 314,*
translated by Joseph W. Trigg, Volume 141 (2020)

ST. AMBROSE, *Treatises on Noah and David,* translated
by Brian P. Dunkle, SJ, Volume 140 (2020)

RUFINUS OF AQUILEIA, *Inquiry about the Monks in Egypt,*
translated by Andrew Cain, Volume 139 (2019)

ST. CYRIL OF ALEXANDRIA, *Glaphyra on the
Pentateuch, Volume 2: Exodus through Deuteronomy,* translated
by Nicholas P. Lunn, Volume 138 (2019)

ST. CYRIL OF ALEXANDRIA, *Glaphyra on
the Pentateuch, Volume 1: Genesis,* translated by
Nicholas P. Lunn, with introduction by Gregory K. Hillis,
Volume 137 (2018)

WORKS OF ST. JOHN CHRYSOSTOM
IN THIS SERIES

Commentary on Saint John, the Apostle and Evangelist: Homilies 1–47,
translated by Sr. Thomas Aquinas Goggin, SCH,
Fathers of the Church 33 (1957)

Commentary on Saint John, the Apostle and Evangelist: Homilies 48–88,
translated by Sr. Thomas Aquinas Goggin, SCH,
Fathers of the Church 41 (1959)

Discourses Against Judaizing Christians, translated by Paul W. Harkins,
Fathers of the Church 68 (1979)

On the Incomprehensible Nature of God, translated by Paul W. Harkins,
Fathers of the Church 72 (1984)

*Apologist: Discourse on Blessed Babylas and Against the Greeks.
Demonstration Against the Pagans that Christ Is God,* translated by
Margaret A. Schatkin, Fathers of the Church 73 (1985)

Homilies on Genesis 1–17, translated by Robert C. Hill,
Fathers of the Church 74 (1986)

Homilies on Genesis 18–45, translated by Robert C. Hill,
Fathers of the Church 82 (1990)

Homilies on Genesis 46–67, translated by Robert C. Hill,
Fathers of the Church 87 (1992)

On Repentance and Almsgiving, translated by Gus George Christo,
Fathers of the Church 96 (1998)

Consolation to Stagirius, translated by Robert G. T. Edwards,
Fathers of the Church 149 (2024)